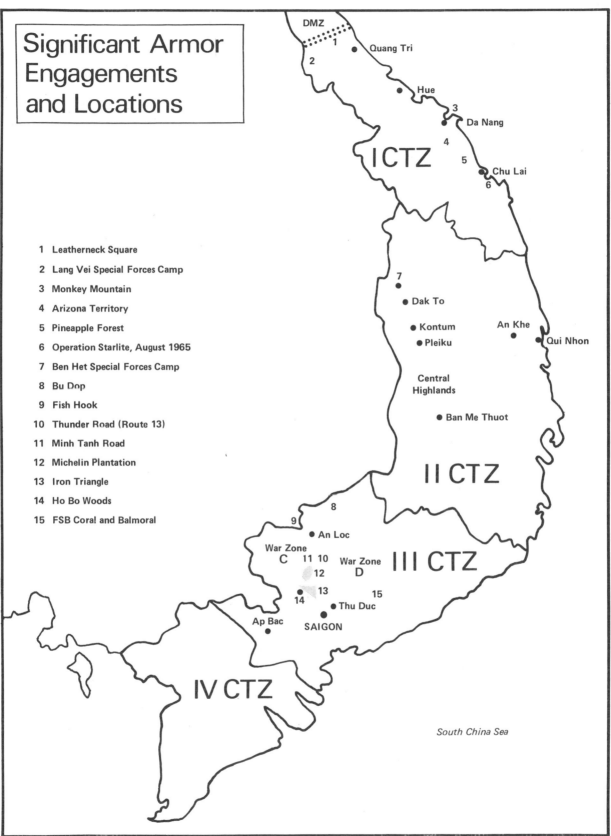

Significant Armor Engagements and Locations

1 Leatherneck Square

2 Lang Vei Special Forces Camp

3 Monkey Mountain

4 Arizona Territory

5 Pineapple Forest

6 Operation Starlite, August 1965

7 Ben Het Special Forces Camp

8 Bu Dop

9 Fish Hook

10 Thunder Road (Route 13)

11 Minh Tanh Road

12 Michelin Plantation

13 Iron Triangle

14 Ho Bo Woods

15 FSB Coral and Balmoral

DMZ

Quang Tri

Hue

Da Nang

Chu Lai

I CTZ

Dak To

Kontum

Pleiku

An Khe

Qui Nhon

Central Highlands

Ban Me Thuot

II CTZ

An Loc

War Zone C

War Zone D

III CTZ

Thu Duc

SAIGON

Ap Bac

IV CTZ

South China Sea

VIETNAM TRACKS

Simon Dunstan

VIETNAM TRACKS

Armor in Battle 1945–1975

Published in the United States by
Presidio Press, 31 Pamaron Way,
Novato, CA 94947

Library cataloging data

Dunstan, Simon
    Vietnam Tracks: Armor in Battle 1945–75
    1. Armored vehicles, Military
    2. Vietnamese conflict, 1961–75—Tank warfare
    3. Vietnam—History—1945–75
    I. Title
    623.74′75′0959704342   UG446.5

    ISBN 0-89141-171-2

Filmset and printed in England
by BAS Printers Limited,
Over Wallop, Hampshire

CONTENTS

Dedication
To R. & W.F.D.

FOREWORD

The considerable effort of Simon Dunstan in addressing the complex subject of armor in South-East Asia merits high praise. He has examined this special armor experience in some detail, and his research coverage is quite professional and complete. His total effort must be considered not only contributory to the study of armor in the Vietnam War, but also—and perhaps more importantly—to its capabilities and limitations in a counter-guerilla environment which those who practice the profession of arms may well come to experience again.

As an armor officer privileged to command the largest American armor unit active in Vietnam at the height of our national involvement, I wish to record certain aspects of tactical employment which I found significant. While most of these points have been well covered by the author, some expansion may be useful to those who may face a similar scenario.

The requirement for good intelligence in all its forms is eternal. I emphasise the word 'good', as opposed to 'superior' or 'perfect': the habitual fluidity of enemy activity in Vietnam absolutely precluded long and detailed study and lengthy intelligence estimates at the tactical level. Quick reaction governed the day: for if one delayed in order to attain just a bit more confirmation of hostile movement one would probably miss the boat. In this connection, nearly all actions in that war commenced with a classic 'movement to contact'. This movement was based on good intelligence, and involved the integrated deployment of air and ground cavalry elements. In my view, and to emphasise this point, the scout helicopter employed in co-ordination with other intelligence resources (some of which were quite highly classified) was the key to success in battle. This applies to upwards of 90 per cent of the actions with which I enjoy some degree of familiarity.

Once the battle was joined, offensive violence coupled with the concentration of firepower and—of vast importance—encirclement, represented the underpinnings of success. The commander's ability to improvise frequently paid dividends. The need for instantly available and continuous pressure forces, employed to prevent enemy withdrawal, was paramount. Again and again the air cavalry scout and, to a slightly lesser degree, committed ground reconnaissance elements played a vital role as the eyes and ears of the armor. The intelligently and carefully employed resources of gunships, tanks and ACAVs could then bring success, and usually did. The slogan 'If you can hold him, you can kill him' applied on most occasions. The major challenge was posed by our occasional inability to prevent the enemy from dispersing from the objective area; and this depended upon how much committable combat power the commander retained in his 'box of tricks'.

Bomb damage assessment operations pursued in conjunction with B52 'Arc Light' strikes—classically speaking, the follow-up of overwhelming firepower with quick-reaction armored and air cavalry units—brought major dividends even against a tricky and capable enemy. This form of operation should neither be forgotten nor dismissed.

My third point relates to the understanding of the term 'armor'. This does not apply simply to a tank, an ACAV or a Sheridan, a helicopter, or a mechanised infantry force. It implies the employment of an acceptable mixture of air and mobile ground units directed, with as much violence as possible, at a hostile target. Although one of the primary gains realised in Vietnam was the effective employment of Army aviation, its role continues to be clouded with uncertainty in some areas. We now see two relative newcomers to the battlefield: the attack helicopter, and the aero scout. Both are armor proponent vehicles employed in basically similar fashion to their older ground counterparts. Within a unit which has a cavalry reconnaissance and security mission, the gunship's role is to support the scout. Within an attack configuration, the gunship becomes the primary element, and the task of the scout becomes the support of the more heavily armed aircraft. In other words, the scout acquires appropriate targets which the attack craft then engages. The Vietnam scenario placed the scout in the primary role, while the attack ship offered its very considerable support. The roles and missions of scout vehicles and tanks in ground armor or armored cavalry units are startlingly similar.

Logistical arrangements also require a word here. Armor must have, in this and perhaps in other and more conventional environments, direct-support maintenance and supply units immediately available and finely tuned to the special 'customer needs'. The development of realistic usage factors for these complex and terrain-sensitive weapons is critical. It follows that supporting formations must be equipped with a preponderance of tracked vehicles, close at hand and promptly responsive to operational demands. This enhances mobility by permitting commanders to cut loose from their supporting bases and to project armored combat power in every operational area.

Mines!

Be on your guard for the enemy's mine warfare capability. Of all the weapons used against the armored units with which I had the good fortune to be associated, this small box of explosives, randomly but effectively placed, gave me the greatest cause for concern. Viet Cong/NVA mine employment was extremely effective, and caused at least 50 per cent of my AFV losses. The Free World must find a better way of dealing with this weapon.

Almost since the advent of armor, its capability to damage and destroy has been persistent and vexing, especially within the context of random employment by the Communist enemy. We must study this technique and improve our own ability to use it effectively. Since the Second World War less progress has been made in mine and countermine doctrine and equipment than in any other single area of land combat.

And finally, the basic, all-too-familiar armor principles of firepower, mobility and shock action pertained in Vietnam as on every other battlefield. They will continue to apply, irrespective of local conditions of terrain, weather, and the identity and nature of the enemy.

In closing, permit me to urge those who maintain an interest in the profession of arms to examine this volume closely. Your improved understanding of what was done, and why, during that tragic but vitally important period of history will provide lessons as to how the armor team can and should come to grips with a Vietnam-type scenario. The lesson is here to be learned; and, as always, the stakes remain high.

George S. Patton
Major General
US Army, Retired

1 FRENCH ARMOR IN INDO-CHINA

In the aftermath of the Second World War, the victorious European powers re-asserted dominion over their colonies lost to the Axis. At the Potsdam conference in July 1945 the responsibility for disarming the Japanese in Indo-China below the 16th Parallel was vested in the British, while to the north it lay with Vietnam's traditional enemy China in the guise of Chiang Kai-Shek's Nationalist army.

On 2 September 1945 the independent Democratic Republic of Vietnam was proclaimed in Hanoi by an elderly schoolmaster named Ho Chi Minh. During the weeks that followed, the nascent Viet Minh government was overwhelmed by the forces of Britain and China. Favouring the restoration of French rule, the British ousted the Viet Minh in Saigon with the aid of armed Japanese units.

During October, units of the French Expeditionary Corps under the command of Lt. Gen. Leclerc landed in Saigon with orders to re-occupy French Indo-China. The first armored unit to arrive was the *Groupement de Marche de la 2e Division Blindée* drawn from the formation commanded by Gen. Leclerc during 1944–5. Known as '*Groupement Massu*' after its commanding officer, it comprised a reconnaissance squadron of M8 armored cars, a squadron of M5A1 light tanks and a provisional infantry unit mounted in half-tracks.

In the following months other units of the *Arme Blindée et Cavalerie* (ABC) arrived, but several lacked AFVs and fought as infantry until they were equipped with vehicles supplied by the departing British. By February 1946 all of southern Indo-China was re-occupied. Following the March agreements with the Viet

M5A1 tanks of the Foreign Legion's 4e Escadron, 1er Régiment Étranger de Cavalerie are refuelled during Operation 'Sauterelle' near RC1, August 1952. The numeral '1' identifies the squadron commander's tank. (ECPA A52/148/8)

When armored units arrived in Indo-China, most roads had disintegrated due to lack of maintenance during the Second World War. Those few bridges that survived were not suitable for AFVs. An M5A1 of 'Groupement Massu' bypasses a destroyed bridge on the road to Ninh Hoa, January 1946. The markings identify the 4e Compagnie, 501er Régiment de Chars de Combat. This unit, together with personnel of 12e Chasseurs and 12e Cuirassiers, formed the tank squadron of 'Groupement Massu'. In accordance with standard French practice, AFVs were named after places and battle honours. (ECPA T11066/G10)

Minh, France recognised North Vietnam, comprising Tongkin and Annam, as an autonomous member of the 'Indo-Chinese Federation' within the French Union. In return the French obtained approval for a military presence in the north for five years and French units rapidly seized control of the region. Further talks between France and Ho Chi Minh failed to reach agreement about the future status and constitution of Vietnam, and the Viet Minh resumed hostilities on 18 December 1946. The First Indo-China War had begun in earnest.

At the outset French armored units were employed for the most part on convoy escort and route security. They were equipped with American and British vehicles used during the Second World War. Although none were designed for the theatre of operations, all proved serviceable against an unsophisticated enemy lacking effective anti-tank weapons. The fundamental limitation was the lack of a suitable troop transport with cross-country mobility. Infantry moved either on foot or in unarmored trucks which were confined to the few arterial roads. Since the French lacked the essential mobility to carry the fight to the elusive Viet Minh, roads determined the axes of advance, while the enemy was free to roam the countryside.

In an effort to provide mobility across the inundated rice paddies and swamps that abounded in the Mekong and Red River Deltas, amphibious units were formed and equipped with M29C Weasel cargo carriers, nicknamed *Crabes* (Crabs) by the French. These vehicles had been employed in limited numbers by infantry and artillery units for medical evacuation and resupply with only marginal success. The *Ier* and *2e Escadrons* of the *Ier Régiment Étranger de Cavalerie* (Ier REC) tested the vehicles in the *Plaine des Joncs* (Plain of Reeds) west of Saigon in December 1947. At first results were disappointing, but the crews quickly developed suitable tactics and the *Crabes* soon proved highly successful. The *Ier Groupe*

Route security and convoy escort were the primary roles of armored units at the outset of the campaign; tasks well suited to the armored cars supplied by the British. A Coventry Mk. I armored car of 5ᵉ Régiment de Cuirassiers 'Royal-Pologne' protects traffic plying a road in Cochin-China, 1951. (ECPA CoC51/19/16)

OPPOSITE ABOVE
In order to reduce losses of men and vehicles from ambushes, armored GMC trucks were used as troop transports, but the increased weight reduced mobility considerably on the marginal roads of Indo-China. The rear floor was not armored but fitted with a thick rubber mat as protection against mines. The tarpaulin acted as an anti-grenade screen. (ECPA L51/19/R1)

OPPOSITE BELOW
An M3A1 Scout Car of 5ᵉ Régiment de Spahis Marocains patrols a track in Cambodia, 1950. Note the five-pointed Allied star of Second World War vintage crudely modified into the regimental badge of 5ᵉ RSM. Armament is a Chatellerault 7.5mm M1931 machine gun with its characteristic drum magazine. The vegetation acted as a sunshield as well as camouflage. (ECPA CA50/4/4)

d'Escadrons du 1ᵉʳ REC extended its field of operations throughout the Mekong Delta, fulfilling long range reconnaissance tasks. The results were so encouraging that further *Crabe* squadrons were formed, but one major tactical limitation remained: the lack of infantry support. Infantry units were too slow to exploit the intelligence gained, and attempts to incorporate an infantry platoon in each *Crabe* squadron proved unsatisfactory because their numbers were insufficient and the vehicles became hopelessly overloaded.

A solution was found among the range of American vehicles that arrived in 1950, which included the Landing Vehicle Tracked (LVT), known as the *Alligator*. A platoon of *Alligators* carrying infantry was incorporated into each *Crabe* squadron. On 1 September 1951 the amphibious units were re-organised becoming the *1ᵉʳ Groupement Autonome* (1ᵉʳ GA). The new formation was now tactically independent of 1ᵉʳ REC, but the légionnaires maintained the regiment's traditions together with its standard and insignia. At the same time, the *2ᵉ Groupement Autonome* was formed for operations in Tongkin.

With the outbreak of the Korean War the American attitude towards France's involvement in Indo-China altered. It was no longer perceived as a colonialist war but as a containment of Communist expansion. American military aid increased dramatically. The ageing M5A1 Stuart light tanks were superseded by M24 Chaffees. The M24 proved highly successful—reliable, well-armed and with a low ground pressure, it exhibited excellent cross-country mobility. It could be driven almost everywhere during the dry season, and even across flooded rice paddies.

The primary task of armored units remained the security of lines of communication, but increasingly they served as reaction forces. French troops were dispersed in small isolated outposts, known as 'hedgehogs', which became highly vulnerable as Viet Minh forces grew in strength. The Communist victory in China during 1949 assured a safe haven and a ready source of military assistance to the Viet Minh. Armored units were deployed at short notice to the aid of besieged outposts or units trapped in ambushes. Such operations

RIGHT
Much of the equipment used by the French in the initial stages of the campaign was supplied by the British, either from the stocks of 14th Army or surplus American Lend-Lease material. Armed with a water-cooled .30 cal. Browning machine gun, this Universal Carrier of the Régiment d'Infanterie Coloniale du Maroc served in Cochin-China in 1951. (ECPA CoC51/10/L3)

OPPOSITE
*Vehicles of GB2 pause on a winding narrow road during Operation 'Tulipe', 1951. Typically of the roads in Indo-China, there was hardly room for even two vehicles to pass each other. Unpaved and bordered by dense undergrowth, these roads were constantly subjected to mining and ambushes. These M24 Chaffees of 2ᵉ Escadron, 1ᵉ RCC carry US white stars indicating their recent arrival under the American Mutual Defense Assistance Program. Légionnaires of III/5ᵉ Régiment Étranger d'Infanterie ride on the rear decks of the tanks.
(ECPA T51/173/124)*

ABOVE RIGHT
*Towing an ammunition limber, an M8 HMC of 1ᵉʳ Régiment de Chasseurs à Cheval negotiates a gully on the road between Son Tay and Trung Ha, 1951. A standard Viet Minh anti-tank tactic was to impress local inhabitants to dig a series of deep ditches at regular intervals across two-thirds of a road, first from one side and then from the other. This allowed peasant bicycles and buffaloes to use the road but blocked the progress of tanks and wheeled vehicles. The French called these ditches 'les touches de piano'—the piano keys. With no tankdozers and few engineer bulldozers available, they were a formidable obstacle, often stretching for several kilometres. The M8 HMC was popular for its speed of response in countering ambushes and its facility for high-angle indirect fire which the tanks did not possess; however, its high ground pressure confined most of its movement to roads, and it was mainly used by reconnaissance units.
(ECPA T51/12/6)*

became ever more hazardous, as the Viet Minh often made diversionary attacks against isolated posts in order to lure armored units into ambushes.

From the beginning Viet Minh anti-tank tactics were based on ambushes and the widespread use of mines. The majority of vehicle casualties were caused by the latter, which ranged from unexploded artillery and aircraft ordnance to conventional Chinese anti-tank mines. As the war progressed the Viet Minh employed greater numbers of portable anti-tank weapons, principally 57mm and 75mm recoilless rifles and bazookas supplied by the Chinese from American equipment captured in Korea. The Viet Minh also produced an effective recoilless rifle, the *Sung Khong Giat* (SKZ) but relatively few AFVs were lost to these weapons. Ambushes invariably occurred in difficult terrain where vehicles had no freedom of movement. A mine was detonated under a vehicle, immobilising those following, which were then attacked by intensive recoilless rifle fire or by Viet Minh sappers wielding Molotov cocktails and satchel charges. After a short, savage firefight the enemy withdrew rapidly to avoid retaliation from French air and artillery fire. On many occasions secondary ambushes were laid for relief forces.

The Viet Minh made extensive use of impressed labour to build obstacles to hamper the movement of French motorised units. Ditches, walls and barricades were constructed across roads and around strongpoints. At times, complete villages were encircled with high earthen ramparts. These obstacles proved very effective and were only overcome by herculean and time-consuming effort, as the French possessed neither tankdozers nor bridge-layers.

Following the rapid re-occupation of Indo-China by fast-moving motorised columns exploiting the limited road network, it became necessary to extend the struggle to the hinterland away from the roads and trails. The strategy adopted by the French was to hold vital points with minimum forces and to concentrate maximum fighting

Over 80 per cent of the vehicles damaged or destroyed were the victims of mines. Generally, AFVs were attacked with command-detonated mines, but hulls were rarely ruptured and crew casualties were few. Maintenance personnel were able to repair such damage in a relatively short time, but were severely hampered by a logistical system that suffered supply delays of six months to a year. (ECPA NVN54/10/19)

ABOVE LEFT
A remanufactured M4A2 Sherman of the Régiment Blindé Colonial d'Extrême-Orient advances along a jungle trail in support of 5e Bataillon de Parachutistes Coloniaux during the battle of the Black River, December 1951. The 75mm gun of the Sherman gave no advantage over that of the Chaffe, while its higher ground pressure restricted mobility on soft terrain. (ECPA T51/210/126)

BELOW LEFT
The shortage of equipment throughout the campaign dictated that even obsolescent AFVs were employed in less critical sectors. A Panhard et Levassor Type 178B armored car mounting a 47mm SA35 cannon in an FL1 turret, patrols a trail during Operation 'Karamaso' in Cambodia, June 1952. Note, again, turret insignia of 5e RSM; this car served with the 1er Escadron. (ECPA CA52/123/91)

power into mobile reserves. However, their strength and equipment were inadequate for the task. Armored units were constantly required to support the overburdened infantry battalions while at the same time maintaining lines of communication throughout the country. Such widespread dispersal frustrated the formation of sufficient armored reserves.

With the arrival as commander-in-chief of General de Lattre de Tassigny, armored units were re-organised in 1951. The first two Sous-groupements Blindées (GB) were formed during the year. These groups comprised a small headquarters, one squadron (escadron) of tanks in four platoons (pelotons), each with three tanks and two half-tracks, and two mechanised infantry companies mounted in half-tracks. At the same time reconnaissance units (groupes d'escadrons de reconnaissance) were organised. These were composed of one tank squadron, one armored car troop of three platoons each with five M8 armored cars, and one platoon of three M8 75mm self-propelled howitzers. These units also contained native infantry: from 1948 the French had begun to employ locally enlisted soldiers. In time, some units were more than 50 per cent Vietnamese, a process known to French troops as 'le jaunissement'—'the yellowing'.

During the same period, mobile strike forces called 'groupements mobiles' (GM) were created. These were composed of up to three infantry battalions mounted in GMC trucks and were supported by a towed 105mm artillery battery, but seldom by more than a platoon or two of tanks. GMs were almost entirely roadbound and therefore prone to ambushes. The necessary close co-operation between infantry and tanks precluded independent armored action, and the tanks often acted merely as mobile artillery. Groupements mobiles became the principal manoeuvre elements of the French Union Forces in the latter years of the conflict.

By the end of 1951 the amphibious units of the two Groupements Autonomes were extensively employed in both the Mekong

Mounting a locally
fabricated machine gun
turret, a Humber Scout Car
Mk. II of the 'Royale-
Pologne' regiment guards a
bridge while protecting a
convoy of 4ᵉ Division
Vietnamien on the road to
Dalat, 1952.
(ECPA A52/104/392)

OPPOSITE ABOVE
An M8 armored car of 3ᵉ
Escadron Blindé
Vietnamien returns fire
during an action in
Tongkin, May 1952. Under
the direction of Gen. de
Lattre national armies were
raised in Vietnam, Laos and
Cambodia during 1950.
Five Vietnamese armored
units and one each in Laos
and Cambodia were
organised and trained. The
formation of these national
forces freed French troops
from static defensive
positions for mobile warfare
against the Viet Minh.
(ECPA T52/125/7)

OPPOSITE BELOW
In November 1950 the
Régiment Blindé Colonial
d'Extrême–Orient
(RBCEO) was formed in
Tongkin and equipped with
M36B2 Tank Destroyers
and Shermans to counter the
threat of Chinese tanks
following the victory of Mao
Tse Tung. M36B2s stand
on the heights of Trung Ha
in the fire support role
during operations along the
Black River, October 1952.
Note the RBCEO insignia
on the turrets.
(ECPA T52/193/14)

and Red River Deltas. Each GA comprised two squadrons each of 33 *Crabes*; three *Alligator* squadrons of 11 LVT4s each and a fire support platoon of six LVT(A)4s. During 1952 1ᵉʳ GA became part of the general reserve, and a new method of employing its amphibious units was adopted. The *Alligators* were used for coastal operations, landings and raids. The latter were generally undertaken by a squadron of *Alligators* and a company of infantry. Being completely amphibious and having the integral fire support of the LVT(A)4 platoon, the units were capable of rapid insertion by sea and were strong enough to undertake a raid some distance inland. Amphibious landings were also conducted as part of larger combined operations. Some such as Operation 'Camargue' in July 1953, which involved elements of ten infantry regiments, two airborne battalions and three armored regiments plus air and artillery support, were on the scale of some assault landings of the Second World War. However, the security of these major operations was often compromised and the enemy frequently withdrew before the arrival of French forces.

Because of the limited successes of these large scale operations, the amphibious units came to be considered too cumbersome, and on 1 April 1953 they were re-formed as 1ᵉʳ and 2ᵉ *Groupements Amphibies*, each comprising three *Groupes d'Escadrons Amphibies* (GEA). Each GEA consisted of one squadron with 15 *Crabes* in three platoons, and one *Alligator* squadron carrying an infantry company. The *Alligator* squadron had eight vehicles comprising one command LVT4, one recovery LVT4, four troop transport LVT4s each with a platoon of infantry, and two LVT(A)4 vehicles for fire support. This organisation gave the amphibious units greater flexibility, and the

ABOVE
Crabes *and* Alligators *of 1er Escadron, 1er Régiment Étrangère de Cavalerie 1er REC) plough through a rice paddy in support of 13e Demi-Brigade de la Légion Étrangère near Tra Vinh during the first operation with LVTs, November 1950. During extended operations in paddyfields the suspension of the* Crabe *tended to become clogged with rice shoots, which overtaxed the relatively fragile mechanism; but with a resourceful crew it proved to have admirable mobility in these formerly inaccessible areas.* (ECPA CoC50/36/60)

BELOW
The crew of a Crabe *of 1er Groupement Autonome man their FM24/29 during Operation 'Crachin' in the Ninh Giang region, February 1952. In 'la guerre sans fronts' attack came from any direction at any time. The* Crabe *was manned by a crew of three or four; standard armament was either a Chatellerault 7.5mm M1924/29 or, more commonly, a Browning .30 cal. M1919A4 machine gun. At this time a* Crabe *platoon comprised eight vehicles: five armed with machine guns, two with 57mm M18A1 recoilless rifles, and one command vehicle. A 60mm mortar was also carried within the platoon. Operation 'Crachin' was named after the cold, misty drizzle that was so prevalent in Tongkin and so evocative of the region.* (ECPA T52/19/3)

ABOVE
KAYZERSBERG, *an* Alligator *of 8e Escadron, 1er REC (2e Groupement Autonome) takes to the water near Haiphong during Operation 'Ouragan', 1952. The usual armament of the* Alligator *comprised two .30 cal. and two .50 cal. Browning machine guns. An M20 75mm recoilless rifle was sometimes mounted at the bow for additional firepower. Locally fabricated gunshields were standard on* Alligators, *and were fitted to many French AFVs.*
(ECPA T52/109/81)

RIGHT
La guerre des grandes vides—*the war of the wide open spaces*: Crabes *of 6e Escadron (6e Sous-Groupement Amphibie) of 1er Groupement Autonome manoeuvre across marshy terrain during Operation 'Quadrille' in Central Annam, July 1952.*
(ECPA A52/128/R9)

ability to engage the enemy more rapidly without losing their ability for independent action.

By the end of 1953 the re-organisation of French armored units to suit the theatre of operations begun in 1951 had been completed and proven in combat. The expanding Vietnamese Army had assumed the role of defending some static positions, allowing the formation of sufficient French reserves for widespread offensive operations. The High Command decided to seek out and engage the Viet Minh in pitched battle in enemy territory. A strong fortress was to be established among the mountains of Tongkin and supplied by air. The choice fell upon a valley surrounded by jungle-covered hills near the Laotian frontier with the innocuous sounding name of 'Seat of the Border County Administration'. In Vietnamese, its name was Dien Bien Phu.

TANKS AT THE BATTLE OF DIEN BIEN PHU

The *base aéro-terrestre* at Dien Bien Phu was conceived as an offensive base from which mobile units and tactical aircraft could strike at the Viet Minh in Northern Tongkin, and as a lure to entice enemy forces from the Red River Delta and Laos to their destruction under the massed firepower of its artillery. To augment its offensive capability, a composite squadron of ten M24 tanks was airlifted to Dien Bien Phu.

Since the French possessed no aircraft capable of transporting an M24, each tank was dismantled into 180 assemblies in Hanoi and the pieces flown into the valley. The shipment of each tank required six C-47 Dakotas, and two Bristol freighters with frontal clamshell doors to accommodate the tank hull and turret. Even when stripped of every nut and bolt the hull weighed 176lbs. more than the Bristol's maximum capacity of 4 tons 220lbs. and to enable it to gain sufficient altitude over the mountains of Tongkin many components had to be removed from the aircraft to reduce weight.

Operation 'Rondelle II' began on 16 December 1953 when légionnaires of 2ᵉ CREBLE set up an assembly area for the tanks

23

LEFT
The mobility of the M24 Chaffee proved highly satisfactory in Indo-China, even during the wet season. A Chaffee of 1ᵉʳ Régiment de Chasseurs à Cheval negotiates waterlogged terrain near Trung Ha during Operation 'Lorraine', October 1952. Operation 'Lorraine' involved a French force of almost 30,000 troops in an attack against a low-lying area known as 'Little Mesopotamia' between the Red and Clear Rivers, where two regiments of the Viet Minh 308th Division were based. Typical of so many operations, 'Lorraine' met with only limited success and failed to achieve its primary objective of forcing large Viet Minh units into a full-scale battle.
(ECPA T52/193/65)

BELOW LEFT
An M2 half-track climbs a 'diguette' (paddy dike) near Phu Nho Quan during Operation 'Mouette' against the Viet Minh 304th Division, November 1953. Half-tracks were employed by mechanised infantry assigned to armored units, but their limited mobility in difficult terrain restricted their movement to paddy dikes, trails and prepared roads where they were susceptible to mines. The canvas tilt acted as an anti-grenade screen.
(ECPA T53/112/59)

ABOVE RIGHT
'Physician heal thyself'— the crew of an International Harvester M5 half-track of 2ᵉ Compagnie Mobile de Réparation de la Légion Étrangère repair their vehicle's suspension before assisting an M5A1 of 6ᵉ Escadron, 1ᵉʳ REC during August 1953.
(ECPA A53/64/6)

beside the airstrip. Two days later the first 'skeleton' arrived. Two Chaffees were completed by the 24th; and the first platoon was formed on Christmas Day from personnel of the *Régiment d'Infanterie Colonial dᵘ Maroc*. On 15 January 1954 Operation 'Rondelle II' ended with the completion of the tanks a fortnight ahead of schedule.

They were divided into three platoons of three tanks each and a headquarters tank for the squadron commander, Capitaine Yves Hervouët. The squadron became operational on 20 January and assumed the title *'Escadron de Marche du 1ᵉʳ Régiment de Chasseurs à Cheval'*. It remained attached to 3ᵉ Escadron, 1ᵉʳ RCC for administrative purposes.

The HQ tank and two of the tank platoons under Sergents Carette and Guntz were located in the *'centre de resistance'* at Dien Bien Phu, while the platoon commanded by Lieutenant Henri Prèaud was assigned to strongpoint 'Isabelle', 2½ miles to the south. In accordance with standard French practice the tanks were named after cities, places or battle honours, painted in white capital letters along the turret sides. These names were used as radio callsigns, but to the garrison the tanks were known as 'the Bisons' (the Viet Minh called them 'Oxen').

After a preliminary period of running-in and final adjustments, all of which were carried out under cover of the morning mist or *'crachin'* to avoid revealing their location, the tanks conducted patrols along the valley to familiarise themselves with the terrain. When not in use they were concealed in sandbagged revetments incorporating dug-outs for crews, ammunition and fuel. The tanks first saw combat on 1 February during an action north-west of 'Gabrielle' (each of the French strongpoints was given a girl's name). Thereafter they undertook numerous offensive patrols in conjunction with *'les paras'* on the slopes of the surrounding hills, to engage weapon emplacements invulnerable to French counter-battery fire.

On the afternoon of 13 March the assault on Dien Bien Phu began when the valley floor erupted under a massive artillery barrage which was followed by wave after wave of Viet Minh infantry. 'Beatrice' fell

AUERSTAEDT, *the M24*
Chaffee of Lt. Henri
Prèaud, before and after
application of camouflage
scheme of earth yellow
stripes displayed by the
tanks at Dien Bien Phu.
(Henri Prèaud)

that night; 'Gabrielle', 36 hours later. A counter-attack by tanks and the *1er Bataillon Étranger de Parachutistes* failed to relieve 'Gabrielle' but did extricate the survivors.

The loss of these strongpoints considerably reduced the field of action of the tanks, but they became the shock element in many actions, invariably taking part in counter-attacks and inflicting heavy losses on the enemy. The squadron, whether in the field or in its static positions, was constantly subjected to artillery bombardment. In spite of the revetments maintenance was very difficult, and replenishing with ammunition was only possible by placing the tank over a trench and passing the rounds through the floor escape hatch. Two tanks, DOUAUMONT and NEUMACH were badly damaged by artillery fire, which also caused the majority of crew casualties. Replacements, some of whom had no jump training, were parachuted in on several occasions. Capitaine Hervouët and platoon commander Carette were both wounded but continued to fight until ordered to cease—Hervouët leading the squadron in repeated actions in his tank CONTI with both arms in plaster casts. The crews were forced to travel and fight closed down for hours on end, which was tiring and slowed all movement.

When the tanks acted in a fire support role, ammunition consumption was high. During the battle each tank fired on average 1,500 shells, and in a typical engagement between 60 and 100 rounds. This proved to be the most serious problem encountered by the tanks, because the M24 carried a basic load of 48 rounds. Extra ammunition was carried on the trackguards and rear decks or on the turret floor and in the assistant driver's position. However, this increased the vulnerability of a tank or impeded the normal functioning of its weapons. Another method was to use one tank in

each platoon solely to carry ammunition; but this reduced the effectiveness of the unit, and replenishing the other tanks in combat was hazardous.

Firing so many rounds in such a short time caused problems with the recoil system. By 7 May three guns were out of action for this reason. Apart from this deficiency the 'Bisons' performed admirably throughout the battle. From the tactical point of view, Capitaine Hervouët's gallant squadron played a decisive part in the defence of Dien Bien Phu. Because of their small numbers and their distribution

A 'Bison' of Peloton Ney and légionnaires of the 1er BEP clear a Viet Minh trench during a counter–attack around 'Eliane 4' on 25 March. (ABC)

In a classic example of 'Débrouille-toi', the Foreign Legion's traditional mastery of improvisation, légionnaires of 2ᵉ Compagnie de Réparation d'Engins Blindés de la Légion Étrangère painstakingly reassemble the M24 Chaffees beside the dusty, windblown airstrip at Dien Bien Phu. (ABC)

between two widely separated positions it was never possible to employ more than six tanks in any one action. Nevertheless, in the determination of its attacks, the accuracy of its fire support and the risks taken in assisting other arms, the conduct of the squadron was outstanding, and in the highest traditions of cavalry.

The courage of the tenacious defenders and the grievous suffering of their wounded was to no purpose. Dien Bien Phu was overwhelmed on 7 May. All the tanks, without exception, were destroyed by their crews that evening.

THE BISONS OF DIEN BIEN PHU
Escadron de Marche du 1ᵉʳ Régiment de Chasseurs à Cheval

Squadron Headquarters Tank. Capitaine Yves Hervouët (1ᵉʳ RCC): WiA, 31 March.

CONTI—	Badly damaged by mine on 5 April during counter-attack at 'Huguette 6'. Recovered and used as pillbox south of the airstrip.

Peloton Carette (RICM). Adjudant-Chef Carette: WiA, 31 March: Platoon under command of Sergent Boussrez from 2 April until 5 April, when Sous-Lieutenant Mengelle took command.

MULHOUSE—	Bazooka'd in turret during counter-attack at 'Eliane II' on 31 March, but continued to fight and remained serviceable to the end.
BAZEILLES—	Bazooka'd in same action as MULHOUSE; burnt out and abandoned.
DOUAUMONT—	Received direct hit from 105mm shell which penetrated assistant driver's position killing three crewmen, 29 April. Used as pillbox at 'Huguette 3'.

Peloton Guntz (1ᵉʳ RCC). Sergent Guntz: KiA, 15 March. Became Peloton Ney until 5 April, when Maréchal-des-Logis Ney WiA. Chef Landois took command of platoon on 12 April, KiA 15 April. All tanks at CR then under command of S/Lt. Mengelle.

SMOLENSK—	Struck twice by 57mm recoilless rifle fire during action at 'Eliane II', 31 March. Subsequently suffered gearbox failure, and out of action by 7 May.
POSEN—	Bazooka'd in turret on 24 March while securing road to 'Isabelle', but serviceable to the end.
ETTLINGEN—	Struck six times by 57mm recoilless rifle during action at 'Eliane II' on 31 March. Bazooka'd on 5 April, two WiA. Bazooka'd in turret on 15 April, two KiA. Available to the end.

Peloton Prèaud (1ᵉʳ RCC). Strongpoint 'Isabelle'

AUERSTAEDT—	In action to the end.
NEUMACH—	Bazooka'd in turret at Ban Kho Lai on 31 March during sortie from Isabelle. Available to the end.
RATISBONNE—	Hit twice by 105mm shells at Isabelle on 29 April. In action to the end.

The three 'Bisons', (POSEN,
SMOLENSK and ETTLINGEN)
of Peloton Ney lie concealed
in their revetments near Col.
de Castries' headquarters
bunker, as smoke billows
from enemy positions on the
perimeter of the 'centre de
resistance' at Dien Bien
Phu after a napalm attack
by Bearcat fighters; 17
March. (ABC)

Vietnamese infantry disembark from an LVT4 of 6ᵉ Groupe d'Escadrons Amphibies (Iᵉʳ RCC), 2ᵉ Groupement Amphibie during an assault in the Nam Dinh region, June 1954. The standard complement of the LVT was 20 French troops or a complete platoon of indigenous infantry. (ECPA NVN54/90/34)

Throughout the war French armored units suffered from an almost total lack of tank recovery vehicles. This M24 of 2ᵉ Peloton, 2ᵉ Escadron, Iᵉʳ RCC came to grief during Operation 'Gerfaut' in December 1953. It was recovered by the other tanks in the platoon attached together in a chain by tow cables. On occasions, as many as a dozen tanks pulling in concert were necessary to extricate a mired vehicle in this way. (ECPA T53/147/87)

Piled with folding cots and ammunition boxes, M24 Chaffees of 2ᵉ Escadron, Iᵉʳ Régiment de Chasseurs à Cheval act as a rearguard during the evacuation of My Coi, July 1954. By this time full-strength tank platoons had four rather than three tanks, so the numeral '14' identifies the leader's tank of 4ᵉ Peloton. (ECPA NVN54/96/45)

Although the fall of Dien Bien Phu was a serious blow to the French cause, it was not a military catastrophe. Less than five per cent of the French Union Forces were lost; but the outcome, like that of the Tet offensive 14 years later, had far-reaching consequences. The French people were weary of '*la sale guerre*'. The defeat broke the political will of the government in Paris to prosecute the war further, and deprived it of bargaining power at the conference convened in Geneva to seek a settlement of the conflict.

Meanwhile the fighting continued in Indo-China, where many areas were stripped of French troops to replace the losses in Tongkin. In Cochin-China the defence of the Mountain Plateau region lay with a single regimental task force, *Groupement Mobile 100*. During the six months of its existence GM100 covered almost 2,000 miles through enemy-dominated territory, continually harassed by the Viet Minh until it was eventually destroyed in repeated ambushes at the time of the ceasefire.

The fate of GM100 was to cast a long shadow, for it greatly influenced American military thinking on the use of armor in Vietnam. To many casual observers it seemed to prove the impossibility of armored operations in jungle warfare. In fact, GM100 was not an armored unit but was composed of truck-mounted infantry with only one squadron of M5A1s in support. Confined to movement on roads, GM100 was vulnerable to ambushes which gradually but inexorably whittled it away to nothing. Nevertheless, its destruction generated among the US Army considerable prejudice against using armor in South-East Asia which persisted for many years.

In Tongkin the Viet Minh were encroaching on the Red River Delta as they systematically eradicated one position after another in what the French called '*le pourrissement*'—'the rotting-away'—until even Hanoi was threatened. Despite the determination and professionalism of the French Army the situation was hopeless, as it proved impossible to contain the enemy. On 20 July 1954 the Geneva Agreements were signed and a ceasefire became effective on the following day.

In the nine years of warfare French armored units had displayed great skill and had acquitted themselves well. However, their lack of numbers led to excessive fragmentation and widespread dispersal which limited their effectiveness. In 1954 French AFVs numbered 452 tanks and tank destroyers and 1,985 armored cars, half-tracks and amphibious vehicles spread over a quarter of a million square miles. By comparison, US forces in Vietnam during June 1969 had some 600 tanks and 2,000 other AFVs deployed over an area less than one-third that size.

By the Geneva Agreements, France lost her colonies in South-East Asia and Vietnam was partitioned along the 17th Parallel. On 9 October 1954 the last French troops left Hanoi, which became the capital of the Democratic Republic of Vietnam. By an awful irony, the last tank to leave Hanoi bore across its glacis plate the name ALGERIE. For the next nine years the French Army was to be mired in yet another futile, bloody war.

FRENCH ARMORED UNITS IN INDO-CHINA
L'escadron autonome de reconnaissance de la brigade d'Extrême–Orient.
Arrived 6 February 1946; disbanded 16 December 1947.

Groupe de Marche de la 2e Division Blindée ('Groupement Massu').
First elements arrived 10 September 1945; disbanded 16 November 1946.

1er Régiment de Chasseurs à Cheval. Arrived January 1946; repatriated and disbanded in 1955.

1er Régiment Étranger de Cavalerie. Arrived 4 January 1947; repatriated at end of hostilities.

Le Régiment d'Infanterie Coloniale du Maroc. Arrived 4 November 1945; repatriated at end of 1954.

2e Régiment de Spahis Marocains. Formed on 1 December 1947 from 2e Régiment de Marche de Spahis Marocains of 'Groupement Massu'. Repatriated 30 March 1955.

5e Régiment de Spahis Marocains. Arrived 28 September 1949; disbanded 31 January 1955.

6e Régiment de Spahis Marocains. Arrived 18 February 1949; repatriated in August 1955.

8e Régiment de Spahis Algeriens. Arrived 18 April 1949; disbanded at end of hostilities.

Le Régiment de Marche du 8e Dragons. Arrived 3 November 1945; disbanded 31 July 1946.

4e Régiment de Dragons. Arrived March 1947; repatriated at end of hostilities.

5e Régiment de Cuirassiers 'Royal-Pologne'. Arrived 2 February 1946; repatriated at end of hostilities.

Régiment Blindé Colonial d'Extrême-Orient. Formed November 1950; disbanded February 1955.

FRENCH ARMOR IN INDO-CHINA, JULY 1954
4 Groupes Blindées : GB,8e Spahis; GB2, 1er RCC; GB3, RICM; GB4,6e Spahis.

2 Groupements Amphibies :
    1er Groupement Amphibie (Tourane/Da Nang):
    2e groupe d'escadrons amphibies (2e & 12e escadrons)
    3e groupe d'escadrons amphibies (3e & 13e escadrons)
    7e groupe d'escadrons amphibies (7e & 17e escadrons)

    2e Groupement Amphibie (Haiphong):
    1er groupe d'escadrons amphibies (1er & 11e escadrons)
    4e groupe d'escadrons amphibies (8e & 18e escadrons)
    6e groupe d'escadrons amphibies (1er Régiment de Chasseurs)

3 Groupes d'Escadrons de Réconnaissance : GER1, 1er RCC; GER2, RICM; GER 3, 1er REC.

6 Armored Regiments : 5e R de Cuirs; 4e RD; RBCEO; 2e Spahis; 5e Spahis. Various independent squadrons in Laos and Cambodia, and national army units.

2 ARMOR OF THE SOUTH VIETNAMESE ARMY

M113s of 7th Mechanised Rifle Co. negotiate a rice paddy at speed: August 1962. Note the characteristic posture of the .50 cal. gunners: many Vietnamese soldiers found it impossible to cock the heavy machine gun unless they braced both legs against the hatch coaming or the 'Chrysler mount'. This practice exposed the gunner to an unacceptable degree and led to the introduction of gunshields. (United States Information Service)

A small Vietnamese armored force was created by the French in 1950. By the time of partition it comprised the 3rd Armored Regiment (formerly *3ᵉ Régiment Blindée Vietnamien*) and four separate armored squadrons. In early 1955 the Vietnamese Armor Command was established, and with the creation of the Republic of Vietnam in October it became a part of the Army of the Republic of Vietnam (ARVN). By the end of the year an armored unit was deployed in each of the four military regions.

The equipment was inherited from the French. All of it was of Second World War vintage, and much of it was in poor condition. The principal AFVs were M24 Chaffee light tanks, M8 Greyhound armored cars, M3 half-tracks, M3 scout cars and M8 howitzer motor carriages. Unfortunately the combination of delapidated equipment, tactics that stressed defence, and the piecemeal commitment of AFVs limited the capabilities of the force to convoy escort and static defence of installations. In the latter rôle AFVs were reduced to the level of 'mobile' pillboxes.

With the arrival of American advisers in early 1956 the existing South Vietnamese armored units were re-organised according to US precepts as armored cavalry regiments each comprising two reconnaissance squadrons equipped with M8 armored cars, M3 half-tracks and M3 scout cars, and one squadron of Chaffees. Vietnamese unit nomenclature was retained from the French, whose designations were equated with fighting power rather than on the basis of personnel strength—the method used by the US Army. This meant that a Vietnamese 'regiment' was equivalent in size to an American battalion or squadron (see table below).

From 1957 to 1962 Vietnamese armored units played only a minor role in the conduct of the war. During this period the Viet Minh, who had remained in South Vietnam since the Geneva Agreements, carried out terrorist attacks, established bases and created a widespread intelligence network and political infrastructure. In December 1960 the National Front for the Liberation of South Vietnam (NLF) was formed; ostensibly a coalition of disaffected

UNIT NOMENCLATURE				
ARVN-Australian	*French*	*US Army Armor*	*US Army Cavalry*	*USMC*
Thiet Doan-Regiment	Régiment	Battalion	Squadron	Battalion
Chi Doan-Squadron	Escadron	Company	Troop	Company
Chi Doi-Troop	Peloton	Platoon	Platoon	Platoon

parties against the autocratic rule of President Ngo Dinh Diem it was, in reality, under Communist control from Hanoi. Its military arm was to become known as the Viet Cong.

By late 1961 the military situation in South Vietnam was grave. The Viet Cong were moving at will throughout the country, and even threatened the approaches to Saigon. In the months that followed the US furnished considerable military and civil aid to bolster the flagging Diem regime. Among the equipment delivered to Vietnam was a batch of M113 Armored Personnel Carriers (APCs). It was decided to introduce two company-sized units manned by rifle companies trained in mechanised infantry operations. The Vietnamese Armor Command insisted that the M113s be evaluated by armor personnel, however, and the APCs were sent to the Armor School at Thu Duc north-east of Saigon.

The first consignment of 32 M113 APCs arrived on 30 March 1962. Rather than being manned by well-trained troops, the new units were completed with men selected at random, and only the key rôles were filled by armor personnel. The two units were designated 'mechanised rifle companies' and were formed with 15 APCs apiece. Each company was divided into three troops of three APCs; a

RIGHT
On arrival in Vietnam in September 1962 the second consignment of M113s was painted in a camouflage scheme of purplish brown stripes over the olive drab base colour. The frame for the rifle rest was a non-standard fitting; typical weapons of this period were the M1 and M2 carbines and the BAR. To allow the small Vietnamese to fight mounted from an M113, boards were spaced between the rear seats. (US Army SC602608)

BELOW
Before the development of obstacle-crossing techniques for M113s, bridging assembled from Light Tactical Raft was flown in by Piasecki CH-21c Shawnee helicopters. Here, an M113 of 21st Mechanised Rifle Co. negotiates an irrigation ditch during an operation near Can Tho, while the ungainly 'flying bananas' rest in the background. (United States Information Service)

support troop with four APCs carrying between them three 60mm mortars and three 3.5in. rocket launchers; and a company HQ section of two APCs, one for the company commander and one for maintenance personnel. As only the driver and commander of each M113 was drawn from armor personnel, while the riflemen lacked combat experience, their initial training period was extended from six weeks to nine. The two units were put into the field for the first time on 11 June 1962. The High Command decided to deploy them

in the Mekong Delta to protect Route 4—the vital 'Rice Route' into
Saigon. They were assigned to the ARVN 7th and 21st Infantry
Divisions and were redesignated the 7th and 21st Mechanised Rifle
Companies.

Early operations were conducted in conjunction with troops of the
Civil Guard—provincial soldiers of mediocre quality—and directed
by a higher command with no knowledge of armored tactics. Many
commanders tended to employ the APC merely as a substitute for a
truck, failing to exploit its mobility, shock action and firepower. In
consequence, initial results were disappointing, provoking much
unfavourable comment on the M113. Gradually, however, the two
mechanised rifle companies gained experience through daily
operations against the enemy.

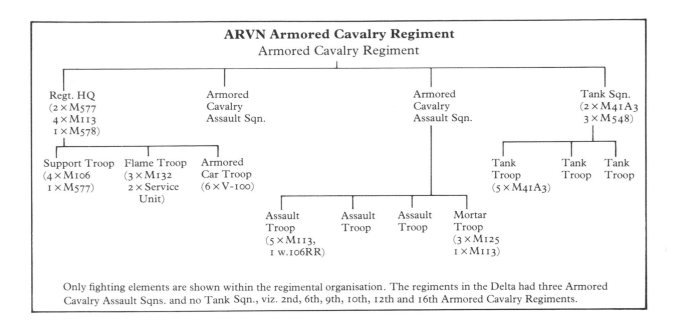

ARVN Armored Cavalry Regiment

Armored Cavalry Regiment

- Regt. HQ
  (2 × M577
  4 × M113
  1 × M578)
  - Support Troop
    (4 × M106
    1 × M577)
  - Flame Troop
    (3 × M132
    2 × Service
    Unit)
  - Armored
    Car Troop
    (6 × V-100)
- Armored
  Cavalry
  Assault Sqn.
- Armored
  Cavalry
  Assault Sqn.
  - Assault
    Troop
    (5 × M113,
    1 w.106RR)
  - Assault
    Troop
  - Assault
    Troop
  - Mortar
    Troop
    (3 × M125
    1 × M113)
- Tank Sqn.
  (2 × M41A3
  3 × M548)
  - Tank
    Troop
    (5 × M41A3)
  - Tank
    Troop
  - Tank
    Troop

Only fighting elements are shown within the regimental organisation. The regiments in the Delta had three Armored Cavalry Assault Sqns. and no Tank Sqn., viz. 2nd, 6th, 9th, 10th, 12th and 16th Armored Cavalry Regiments.

ARVN cavalry troopers and their American advisers devised a number of ingenious techniques for negotiating the innumerable waterways of the Mekong Delta. By means of a block and tackle attached to another carrier on the far bank, an M113 APC crawls over a steep river bank. (Stanley Holtom)

In time, the performance of the M113 in the Plain of Reeds and elsewhere in the Delta demonstrated the effectiveness of the APC as a fighting vehicle—as opposed to its use merely for transporting infantry to the objective. The M113 had been designed as a 'battlefield taxi' following American doctrine that mechanised troops dismount and assault an objective on foot; but operational experience revealed that dismounting infantry prior to closing on a VC position resulted in the loss of momentum, drastically reducing the mobility of ARVN forces and sacrificing armor protection, observation and shock-action effect. Henceforth, ARVN mechanised troops hab-

ABOVE
*As mechanised units
operated more frequently in
areas once dominated by the
Viet Cong, so the enemy
devised counter-measures to
the M113. Large holes
known as 'tiger traps' were
dug to an exact size in
roads. They were sufficiently
wide to prevent vehicles
from manoeuvring across
but too narrow for them to
enter and climb out again.
These simple methods
seriously hampered the
progress of APCs in certain
areas, and led to the
development of a bridgelayer
based on the M113. (Armor
Magazine)*

ABOVE RIGHT
The principal threat to AFVs in Vietnam was the mine. A rupture such as this would have caused fatalities among personnel inside the carrier. For this reason, crews habitually rode on top of M113s. (United States Information Service)

LEFT
Typical damage sustained by an M113 from an RPG-2. The trim vane gave a modicum of 'stand-off' protection to the front of the vehicle. Despite hull penetration, the crew of this vehicle suffered no casualties. (Stanley Holtom)

ARVN Armor Inventory/Establishment 1973								
	Armor School	Armor Brigade (×4)	ACR HQ (×18)	ACAS (×42)	M41 Tank Sqn. (×12)	Tank Regt. HQ (×3)	M48 Tank Sqn. (×9)	TOTAL
M41A3	10				17			214
M48A3	10					3	19	190
M577A1		2	3			5		77
M113A1	18	6	4	18	2	9	1	930
M125A1	3			3				129
M106A1	2		4			4		86
M132A1	2		3					129
XM45E1	1		2					37
M548				3	3		4	198
M88	1					2	1	17
M578	1		1(×12)		1			25
XM806	1		1(×6)	1				49
V-100	12		6					120

itually fought from their carriers, only dismounting when an enemy position had been overrun and then only to ensure that a thorough and complete search of the area was made. The M113 had become a fighting vehicle to be used in a tank-like role, a doctrine subsequently adopted by some American units.

By the end of October, the two companies had killed 517 Viet Cong and captured 203, at a cost to themselves of only four dead and 13 wounded. Such impressive statistics did much to assuage the Vietnamese political establishment, which put a high premium on holding down casualties in men and equipment. Any commander incurring heavy losses was liable to immediate dismissal, a fact which

hardly engendered an aggressive spirit. Much of the psychological shock effect generated by the use of M113s in areas previously denied to government forces was therefore negated by the temerity of commanders who feared losing vehicles and equipment in sustained actions against the VC. Operations rarely lasted longer than two or three days.

The success of the first two M113 companies, now called Mechanised Rifle Squadrons, led to the formation of six additional M113 squadrons and four reconnaissance squadrons equipped with the M114 Command and Reconnaissance Vehicle. The first two mechanised companies were redesignated 4th and 5th Mechanised Rifle Squadrons and were assigned to 2nd Armored Cavalry Regiment based at My Tho in the Mekong Delta. The existing armored cavalry regiments (1st to 4th) were re-organised in late 1962. M113s for the new squadrons arrived in September 1962, as well as M114s for the reconnaissance units. Training began the following month. By May 1963 re-equipment was complete: each of the four regiments had one tank squadron of M24 Chaffees, one reconnaissance squadron of M114s and two mechanised rifle squadrons equipped with M113s, except for 2nd Armored Cavalry Regiment which had no tank squadron but an additional M113 squadron.

The Reconnaissance Squadron comprised a headquarters of two M114s; three reconnaissance troops, each equipped with six M114s in two three-carrier sections; and additional elements in $\frac{1}{4}$-ton trucks. A total of 80 M114s were acquired to equip the four reconnaissance squadrons that served in 1st to 4th Armored Cavalry Regiments. The M114 was an unsound vehicle and proved to be a failure in Vietnam. Underpowered, mechanically unreliable and with marginal amphibious capability, it proved unable to negotiate the same terrain as the M113, and its resistance to mine damage was pitiful: even a moderate-sized mine would literally blow the vehicle in half. The abject failure of the M114 led to its replacement by the M113 by November 1964.

The M113 meanwhile was found to be an outstanding vehicle,

During the Vietnam War a wide variety of weapons was installed experimentally on M113s. Some, such as recoilless rifles, proved successful and were generally adopted. At first 57mm recoilless rifles were tried in place of the .50 cal. machine gun in support troops, but from this position the backblast proved unnerving, if not actually dangerous, to the rest of the crew. (James Loop)

UH-1B Hueys carrying reaction forces of 7th Regt., 5th Infantry Div., land beside a column of APCs ambushed near Bau Bang in July 1965. Despite many successes, ARVN mechanised units suffered some severe reverses, notably at Ap Bac in January 1963. Typical of enemy tactics, the carriers were halted by mines and RPGs and then attacked with satchel charges.
(US Army SC629847)

ABOVE

Two versions of the V-100 Commando were supplied to ARVN forces, one mounting a combination of .30 and .50 cal. machine guns, and the other twin M1919A4 Brownings. Both were classified as the XM-706, but were called by the Vietnamese 'Xe Commando'. The vehicle illustrated was employed by the headquarters of 1st Armd. Cavalry Regt. and shows the flat driver's hatches and three vision blocks along the side indicative of an early production model. (James Loop)

ABOVE LEFT

M113s of 10th Armd. Cavalry Regt. struggle through a glutinous rice paddy near Sy Doi, June 1967. Two of the APCs carry 15-foot lengths of aluminium balk, while the third is fitted with an M74C machine gun turret. The M4T6 balk was a valuable aid to mobility in difficult terrain. Not only was it used for 'push-bar' extraction, but when bolted together to form pairs of treadways, it could span canals or form a ramp up steep banks. Track shrouds were removed or cut back, front and rear, in the Mekong Delta, where soft mud tended to accumulate under the shrouds until it immobilised the vehicle. (US Army SC661437)

OPPOSITE BELOW

Vietnamese armored units were given the name 'coup troops' by detractors. In the same vein, tanks were called 'voting machines' because they influenced several early changes of government in Saigon. The sensitivity of Vietnamese leaders to this aspect of ARVN armored capability led to counter-productive deployment of units on more than one occasion. Here, M24 Chaffees from the Armor School at Thu Duc assault the presidential palace during the successful coup against Ngo Dinh Diem, 2 November 1963. Rebel tanks were daubed with white blotches to distinguish them from those of the presidential guard (Patton Cavalry Museum)

47

*M113s of 4th Armd.
Cavalry Regt. stand guard
on the streets of Saigon after
the coup d'état that
overthrew the regime of Ngo
Dinh Diem, 3 November
1963. On the previous day
Diem and his brother Nhu
were assassinated in the back
of an M113 of the 4th
ACR. Two of these APCs
are fitted with M74
turrets mounting twin
.30 cal. machine guns.
(US Army SC607331)*

capable of cross-country movement previously unrealised in many areas of the Republic. In the Delta the principal obstacles to APC movement were the numerous irrigation canals and rivers. Various techniques were devised for canal crossing and vehicle recovery, among them the use of push-bars, demolition, brush fill, block and tackle, multiple tows and expedients for self-recovery such as the capstan and anchor.

New organisations, tactics and techniques, as well as new items of equipment were tested in combat throughout the country during 1963. Among the modifications made to M113s at this time was the fitting of a gunshield to the .50 cal. machine gun. The deaths of at least 14 .50 cal. gunners at the battle of Ap Bac I in January 1963 impelled the provision of greater protection. The first gunshields were fabricated locally from whatever materials were at hand. 2nd Armored Cavalry Regiment made some of soft steel plating from the

ABOVE RIGHT
During the Buddhist revolt of May 1966 there occurred one of the most remarkable incidents of the war involving AFVs, when M41A3 tanks of 5th Armd. Cavalry Regt. were airlifted from Saigon directly into combat at Da Nang. One quarter of the entire worldwide inventory of USAF C133 Cargomasters was concentrated at Tan Son Nhut airbase. Each C133 carried two fully combat-loaded M41A3s, complete with crews riding at their positions inside the tanks in order not to disturb the critically calculated centre of gravity of the aircraft. On arrival in Da Nang the tanks rolled down the ramps straight into a firefight. The presence of the tanks was instrumental in rallying loyalist forces and quelling the mutiny in I Corps—a further instance of armored troops affecting the political situation in Vietnam. For this reason, this brilliant example of American expertise in strategic mobility has never been accorded the prominence it deserves, as the State Department severely reprimanded those Americans partaking in the operation for what it perceived as unacceptable interference in Vietnamese domestic politics. An M41A3 of 1/5 Armored Cavalry reverses into the belly of a Cargomaster at Tan Son Nhut airbase at the outset of the airlift. (Private collection)

49

OPPOSITE TOP
*When the M24 was replaced by the M41A3 in 1965, the redundant Chaffees were stripped of their engines and placed around important installations as static pillboxes manned by militia troops. Two 'flights' of five M24s each were stationed at Tan Son Nhut airbase. The prime minister, Air Marshal Ky, mindful that armored units had overthrown his predecessors, forbade the removal of the engines of these particular tanks and required air force crews to operate them so as to maintain a counter-coup force. Here USAF security police and an M24 search for VC sappers during the Tet assault on the base, 31 January 1968.
(US Air Force K32017)*

OPPOSITE BELOW
*An ARVN Commando armored car accompanied by military police fires into BOQ3 (Bachelor Officers' Quarters), one of several American installations in Saigon—including the Embassy—attacked by the Viet Cong during the Tet offensive, 31 January 1968.
(US Army SC644455)*

ABOVE
In the Tet offensive of 1968 ARVN armored units conclusively demonstrated their effectiveness, and were a significant factor in the military defeat inflicted on the Viet Cong. As battle rages in the streets of Saigon, M41A3 tanks and M113 APCs engage enemy strongpoints, 31 January 1968. (Armor Magazine)

hull of a sunken ship, but when it was discovered that these could be penetrated other versions were made from the plate of redundant armored vehicles, mainly M3 half-tracks and scout cars. One crew of 4th Armored Cavalry Regiment at Da Nang even fashioned a gunshield from the bumper of a worn-out fork-lift truck. The ARVN 80th Ordnance Depot in Saigon quickly developed the idea and produced drawings and specifications for a standard gunshield. From 1964 these were fitted to all APCs before being issued to ARVN forces. ARVN units also mounted M1919 .30 cal machine guns, some with shields but most without, on the sides of APCs to increase firepower. Many APCs were fitted with machine gun turrets mounting twin .30 cal guns in place of the .50 cal. These cupolas were popular with ARVN troops, but the .30 cal. was inferior to the .50 for penetrating earth and log emplacements, and the latter remained the standard weapon for APCs throughout the war.

By 1964 the superannuated M24 Chaffee inherited from the French had become more of a liability than an effective fighting machine. Spare parts were difficult to obtain and mechanical problems were legion, compounded by the necessity of sending engines to Japan for rebuilding. In mid-1964 the M41A3 Walker Bulldog light tank was chosen to replace the M24. The first M41A3s arrived in January 1965, and by the end of the year five squadrons were equipped and trained. The M41A3 proved an excellent choice and was popular with the Vietnamese. Its combination of rugged

and a gunshield for the commander's machine gun, August 1968. (James Loop)

RIGHT
The ARVN gave no designation to their M113s configured as fighting vehicles with side-mounted Brownings and gunshields. Unlike American ACAVs, the vehicle commander did not man the .50 cal. machine gun but rode in the troop compartment; here he sits behind the driver. This photograph shows the 'belly armor' extending up the lower hull front and the floatation cells that were fitted to compensate for the extra weight. (Armor Magazine)

LEFT
One of the methods devised by M113 units for crossing muddy rice paddies was the 'daisy-chain' or 'choo-choo train'. A number of APCs were cabled together and all the vehicles pulled in concert, so that a vehicle that bogged down would be drawn along by the others. The lack of recovery vehicles capable of operating with M113s in waterlogged areas led to this method being used to extricate vehicles stuck in the mud. Here, an M132A1 'Zippo' leads a 'daisy-chain' of carriers from 2nd Armored Cavalry across a canal near Can Tho in IV CTZ, February 1969.
(US Army SC649235)

ABOVE
After the Tet offensive of 1968 the organisation of ARVN cavalry units changed to five APCs per troop, giving a total of 22 AFVs in an Armored Cavalry Assault Squadron. From 1970, one APC in each troop was authorised to carry a 106mm recoilless rifle for increased firepower. It was installed on the right-hand side of the vehicle. Recoilless rifles were always mounted to the right, since ARVN cavalry troopers learned early not to expose to the enemy the left-hand side of the APC where the fuel tank was located. Note blue dragon symbol painted forward on the hull side.
(James Loop)

simplicity, mechanical reliability and responsive handling made it a very battleworthy machine. The principal criticism of the tank in US service—cramped crew conditions—did not trouble the smaller Vietnamese. The M41A3 proved to be a potent fighting vehicle in Vietnam and gave admirable service in the hands of ARVN cavalry troopers.

At the outset the Viet Cong were ill-prepared to counter the M113, as this passage from a captured document reveals: 'The enemy APCs appeared while we were weak and our anti-tank weapons were still rare and rudimentary. We had no experience in attacking the APC. Therefore, the enemy's APCs were effective and caused us many difficulties at first.'

Initially the VC fled when confronted with M113s, which they dubbed 'Green Dragons' from their appearance as they moved rapidly over waterlogged paddy fields belching fire and smoke from guns and engines. As time went by, the VC adapted their tactics to meet the menace. Holes were dug in Delta roads. Improvised explosive devices were placed at defiles and obstacle crossing points. Early in 1963 the Viet Cong were issued with HEAT ammunition for the Chinese Type 36 57mm recoilless rifle (copied from the US M18A1 of Korean War vintage) which soon became their principal heavy infantry weapon. During the year other anti-tank weapons were encountered, including the Polish PGN-2 anti-tank grenade fired from the AK-47 assault rifle and the powerful Chicom Type 52 75mm recoilless rifle (copied from the US M20).

As increased use was made of the M113, so VC anti-tank weapons proliferated, and by 1965 they were issued as low as company level in regular and provincial units. Most formidable of the VC armor-defeating weapons was the Soviet RPG-2 and its Chinese derivative, the Type 56. The RPG-2 was superseded by the RPG-7, an improved rocket-propelled grenade of increased lethality and range.

LEFT
Two of the crucial elements in the repulse of the Easter invasion of 1972 were armor and airpower, which included helicopter gunships armed with TOW anti-tank missiles, used for the first time in combat with considerable success. A Huey 'slick' flies low over an M41A3 on the southern edge of Quang Tri city, April 1972. (Patton Cavalry Museum)

BELOW LEFT
The crew of an ARVN M48A3 display their delight at the ceasefire of 28 January 1973. Such jubilation was to be shortlived, as Communist encroachment continued, culminating in the 'Ho Chi Minh' campaign of 1975 and the fall of the Republic of Vietnam. (Patton Cavalry Museum)

The hollow-charge warhead was capable of penetrating considerable thicknesses of armor as long as it struck at or near normal incidence and detonated at the proper stand-off distance. M113s sustained approximately one penetration for every seven RPG hits. Hits in themselves averaged about one in eight to ten rounds fired due to the inherent inaccuracy of the weapon. M41A3 penetrations were proportionally less because of its superior ballistic configuration as compared to the slab-sided M113. Statistical analysis reveals that only one vehicle was destroyed for every seven penetrations and casualties were 0.8 per penetration. Nevertheless, this simple, cheap and effective weapon was a constant and serious threat to allied armor throughout the war.

ARVN ARMORED UNITS 1973

(Dates of activation in parentheses)

MILITARY REGION I
> 4th ACR at Chu Lai (1956)
> 7th and 11th ACR at Dong Ha (1965 & 1968)
> 17th ACR at Hoi An (1969)
> 20th Tank Regiment at Quang Tri (1971)
> I Armor Brigade HQ at Da Nang (1969)

MILITARY REGION 2
> 3rd ACR at An Khe (1954)
> 8th ACR at Ban Me Thuot (1965)
> 14th ACR at Kontum (1969)
> 19th ACR at Pleiku (1971)
> 21st Tank Regiment at Pleiku (1972)
> II Armor Brigade HQ at Pleiku (1971)

MILITARY REGION 3
> 1st ACR at Duc Hoa (1956)
> 5th ACR at Xuan Loc (1963)
> 10th ACR at Cu Chi (1966)
> 15th and 18th ACR at Bien Hoa (both 1969)
> 22nd Tank Regiment at Bear Cat (1972)
> III Armor Brigade HQ at Bien Hoa (1970)
> Armor School at Bear Cat

MILITARY REGION 4
> 2nd ACR at Vinh Long (1956)
> 6th ACR at My Tho (1963)
> 9th ACR at Soc Trang (1966)
> 12th ACR at Can Tho (1968)
> 16th ACR at Long Xuyen (1969)
> IV Armor Brigade HQ at Can Tho (1969)

3 US ARMY ARMOR IN VIETNAM

On 6 March 1965 the Pentagon announced that two battalions of Marines were being sent to South Vietnam at the request of the government in Saigon to assist the ARVN in securing the Da Nang airbase. Two days later Battalion Landing Team 3/9 made an assault landing on Red Beach 2, just north of Da Nang, to be greeted by groups of giggling Vietnamese girls dispensing garlands of red and yellow flowers. In support of BLT 3/9 were the M48A3 tanks of 2nd

An A1 Skyraider swoops low over Task Force Dragoon as an M48A3 retrieves an APC hit by recoilless rifle fire during an ambush by 9th Viet Cong Div. on the Minh Tanh road in which Troops B and C, 1st Sqn., 4th Cavalry routed the enemy on 9 July 1966. The battle of the Minh Tanh Road in War Zone C was one of the first major engagements to demonstrate the ability of armored units to withstand a mass ambush and defeat a numerically superior force through firepower and mobility. (Tim Page)

Platoon, Company B, 3rd Tank Battalion and the Ontos vehicles of 3rd Platoon, Company C, 3rd Anti-Tank Battalion—the first American armored units to be committed to the Vietnam War.

In fact these were not the first US armored units to arrive in the country. During the previous year on 2 November the Viet Cong attacked the American airbase at Bien Hoa near Saigon, killing five Americans and destroying six Martin B-57 (Canberra) bombers. Fearing a similar raid on the Da Nang airbase, 3rd Battalion, 3rd Marine Regiment (3/3 Marines) was landed on 9 December 1964 at Da Nang from an SLF patrolling Yankee Station. Armor support included 3rd Platoon, Company A, 3rd Tank Battalion; 1st Platoon, Company A, 3rd Anti-Tank Battalion and 1st Platoon, Company B, 1st Amphibian Tractor Battalion. Acting as a reaction force, these units remained for a week at a Vietnamese Navy PT base at Monkey Mountain before re-embarking on USS *Thomaston* and sailing for Okinawa.

*'Get some Charlie!'—
firing the .50 cal. and
7.62mm co-ax machine
guns, an M48A3 (Late
Model) of Co. A,
2/34th Armor rakes the
treeline as infantrymen
of the 'Tropic
Lightning' Division
assault Viet Cong
entrenched in a bunker
system. Armor was
fearsomely effective in
the destruction of
fortified positions.
(Armor Magazine)*

The arrival of Marine tanks in March 1965 caused consternation at MACV, where planners had failed to study the composition of a Marine BLT and therefore did not realise that it included tanks. The US ambassador to Saigon, Maxwell D. Taylor, expressed his displeasure at the presence of tanks, deeming them to be 'not appropriate for counter-insurgency operations'. The Marines, for their part, saw no reason to alter their methods of employment, so tanks appeared in Vietnam by default rather than design.

On 22 March, 2nd Platoon, Company A, 3rd Tank Battalion disembarked at Da Nang with 2/3 Marines, to be followed on 10 April by 2nd Platoon, Company C, 3rd Tank Battalion at Phu Bai. For the remainder of the month these three tank platoons bolstered the defences of Da Nang airbase. Their first operational use occurred in the first week of May.

By December, the III MAF tank force consisted of 65 M48A3 tanks and 12 M67A2 flame tanks deployed at three Marine enclaves. In addition to the tanks there were 65 Ontos from both 1st and 3rd Anti-Tank Battalions, and 157 LVTP-5A1 amphibian tractors from 1st and 3rd Amphibian Tractor Battalions attached to Marine infantry units.

The first major battle involving Marine armored units occurred in August during Operation 'Starlite' when three Marine battalions, each supported by a tank platoon, trapped 1st Viet Cong Regiment on the Van Tuong Peninsula, 15 miles south-east of Chu Lai airfield. By 24 August, after six days of bitter fighting, the Marines had killed 614 VC, by body count, taken nine prisoners and captured 109 weapons at a cost of 45 Marines dead and 203 wounded. Seven tanks

M48A3 tanks and ACAVs of 1st Sqn., 1st Cavalry forge across a dry paddy field during a reconnaissance in force, August 1968. C-ration cartons and dirt-filled ammunition boxes were often strapped to the rear top quarter of ACAVs to provide a modicum of protection to the M60 gunners against small arms fire from behind. (US Army SC653220)

and nine amphibian tractors were damaged by enemy fire, but the regimental commander claimed that 'the tanks were certainly the difference between extremely heavy casualties and the number we actually took. Every place the tanks went, they drew a crowd of VC.'

Operation 'Starlite' was one of the first tests of Gen. Westmoreland's evolving strategy of 'search and destroy', whereby US forces sought to engage the Viet Cong in the field rather than remaining passively in coastal enclaves and yielding the initiative to the enemy. Because of strict troop ceilings and a severely limited logistical base, armored units were not seriously considered when the first major deployment of US Army units to Vietnam began in mid-1965. Added to this was a deep-seated army prejudice against tanks. In fact, when 1st Infantry Division arrived in October 1965 it had been stripped of its two tank battalions and all mechanised infantry units, which were organised as dismounted infantry battalions. Only the divisional armored cavalry squadron—1st Squadron, 4th Cavalry—retained its M48A3 tanks. These 27 tanks were allowed by the Department of the Army in order to test the effectiveness of armor, but because of the prevailing 'no tanks in the jungle' attitude at MACV the M48A3s were withdrawn from the cavalry troops and held at the squadron base at Phu Loi. There they remained for six months, until the divisional and squadron commanders finally convinced MACV that tanks could be used on combat operations.

The same fate befell other formations authorised for Vietnam. It was only at the insistence of the commander of 25th Infantry Division that when it arrived in March 1966 it retained its tank and mechanised infantry battalions despite resistance from the Department of the

RIGHT
An M113 APC armed with an automatic grenade launcher—one of several weapons fitted in place of the .50 cal. machine gun to increase the firepower of the M113. (Robert Icks)

BELOW
M113 'Poppa Charlies' of the 'Tropic Lightning' Division move across rice paddies during Operation 'Kolekole', June 1967. The inherent amphibious capability of the M113 proved a major asset in such terrain. Of particular interest, the second vehicle is an XM734, an M113 modified by the addition of four firing ports on either side and two in the rear ramp. This was an early experimental model in the development of a mechanised infantry combat vehicle (MICV) which has led to the infantry fighting vehicle (IFV) of today. The XM734 was tested in Vietnam in limited numbers. However, the hull firing ports proved unpopular during operations and the infantry usually rode on, and fired its weapons from, the top of the APC. (US Army CC40850)

OPPOSITE ABOVE
The standard ACAV configuration is shown here, with the vehicle commander at the .50 cal. machine gun, two M60 gunners, driver, and the fifth crew member acting as ammunition bearer. The minigun box beneath the elbow of the right hand M60 gunner contained readily accessible belts of 7.62mm ammunition,

or else was filled with sand as protection against hostile fire to the rear. Resourceful crews also used these containers as a rudimentary washing machine: if they were filled with soapy water and dirty fatigues at the outset of a day's operation, the constant motion of the vehicle effectively cleaned the clothing by nightfall. Trash bags were hung on the rear of the vehicles to carry the rubbish accumulated on operations for eventual disposal on return to camp, so denying to the enemy a source of drink cans, discharged batteries, etc., for use in boobytraps. (James Loop)

An M113 APC of Co. C, 5th Bn., 60th Infantry of 9th Inf. Div., stands guard as a section of the battalion medical platoon holds a 'MedCap' (Medical Civic Action Program) for the villagers of Ap Tinh Thi, February 1967. Troops were forbidden to ride on APCs with their legs dangling over the sides for the obvious reason that if the vehicle struck a mine the blast could sever exposed limbs. In the background is an 'Eiffel' bridge. (US Army CC38583)

'Charlie Brown' makes a suitably cryptic comment beside an RPG penetration of an ACAV of 3rd Sqn., 5th Cavalry of 9th Inf. Div.; the crew perform repairs to the suspension during Operation 'Junction City', March 1967. The characteristic spalling effect of the RPG clearly shows the angle of attack; such damage was repaired by cutting a square around the hole and inserting a new piece, as the heat of penetration degraded the integrity of the armor over the surrounding area. More often than not the crew simply plugged the hole with whatever was to hand, and carried on until more extensive remedial work could be effected. (US Army SC661456)

'Contact! Standby Dust-off.' ACAVs of Troop B, 1/1st Cavalry return fire during an ambush on Route 9 near Khe Sanh, March 1971. In the 'mad minute' that followed engagement, an armored cavalry platoon could deliver a stupendous volume of fire. Each ACAV carried (depending on unit SOP) in the order of 10,000 rounds of .50 cal. ammunition and 20,000 rounds for each M60, sufficient for ten minutes' firing. As they usually faced the firepower of the tank or Sheridan section also, only the boldest foes would attack an armored unit. The leading ACAV has no gunshields for the side-mounted M60s. Some crews judged ease of handling and visibility to be more beneficial than the armor protection offered by these shields. The absence of markings and personal graffiti is typical of ACAVs in Vietnam. (US Army SC661344)

RIGHT
Sgt. Robert Lagana and men of Troop C, 3/4th Cavalry erect RPG screens in front of their ACAVs while establishing a night defensive position. Each crew dug a foxhole between the vehicles and armed it with a dismounted M60. The PSP (Pierced Steel Planking) along the sides of the ACAVs was laid over the foxholes and covered with sandbags as overhead protection. (Robert Lagana)

APCs of 4th Bn., 23rd
Infantry (Mechanized)
'Tomahawks' of 25th
Inf. Div. move forward
in the 'Dog's Face' area
of Cambodia during the
incursion of 1970. Both
vehicles are fitted with
stand-off armor along
the sides and the second
APC with a side-
mounted .50 cal.
machine gun.
Interestingly, the
leading M113A1 has
its exhaust stack
pointing forward. Not
only did this vent the
hot exhaust gases away
from the crew
compartment, but it
also acted as a useful
indicator to aircraft
when operating in
jungle. Under a blanket
of trees it was difficult
for supporting air to
identify a line of
vehicles in contact; but
if a smoke grenade was
placed in or beside the
exhaust pipe and the
engine gunned, a plume
of coloured smoke rose
vertically through the
thickest growth showing
the exact forward
location of M113s on
the ground. Aircraft
could then attack
without fear of striking
friendly troops.
(Armor Magazine)

Army and MACV. Within weeks these armored units participated in a major operation in the jungle and rubber plantations north of Saigon, proving conclusively the efficacy of armored forces and exploding the myth that tanks could not be used in jungle.

Throughout 1966 other formations complete with their armored elements were deployed to Vietnam. It soon became apparent that armored units were proving far more useful in combat than had previously been thought possible. By early 1967 they included one armored cavalry regiment, two tank battalions, four armored cavalry squadrons, six mechanised infantry battalions and five separate ground cavalry troops. New tactics and techniques were evolved as armored units sought out the elusive enemy. Tactical mistakes led to changes being made in operational procedures, but the mobility and heavy firepower of armored units often compensated for these errors. In time a pattern in armor tactics emerged, and these were codified in a study conducted in early 1967 entitled 'Mechanized and Armor Combat Operations in Vietnam' (MACOV). Its findings prompted Gen. Westmoreland to request more armored and mechanised units and marked the final acceptance by the US Army of armor on the battlefields of Vietnam.

Tactics and Techniques

The contemporary doctrine of combat tactics and techniques employed by American armor and mechanised infantry units in Vietnam was based principally on experience gained during the Second World War and the Korean War. Primarily orientated toward a conventional tactical environment, it remained generally valid in Vietnam, but several significant changes in equipment, organisations and techniques were necessary to apply this basic doctrine under the conditions of weather, terrain and enemy that prevailed.

The nature of the war varied significantly from region to region, reflecting the many factors peculiar to each of the four Corps Tactical Zones. Although terrain and weather gave a characteristic signature

The M577 was
essentially an M113
with a raised roof for
use as a command post.
An auxiliary generator
was mounted on the
front vertical hull plate
to power additional
communications
equipment. Besides its
role as a command post,
the M577 was used as a
communications vehicle
or as an artillery fire
direction centre. This
M577A1 of 11 ACR
carries dirt-filled boxes
along the roof as
protection against
hostile fire to personnel
riding on top. Note the
wheel spacing of the
trailer has been
extended to conform
with the track path of
the APC, so as to
reduce the likelihood of
mine detonation.
(James Loop)

The M577 was also
employed as a Field
Aid Station for the
evacuation or treatment
of battle casualties in
armored units. The
enemy frequently
attacked 'angel tracks',
paying no heed to the
prominent red crosses
which became
convenient RPG
aiming points. In
consequence the red
crosses were obliterated
and many ambulances
were armed for self-
protection. Here, an
M577A1 Field Aid
Station of 2/11 ACR
provides medical
support during a
search-and-clear
mission, January 1967.
(US Army CC41644)

Cause and effect—an ACAV of Troop E, 2nd Sqn., 11 ACR lies burning after hitting a mine on 'Thunder Road' (Route 13), August 1967. The interior photograph leaves little to the imagination as to the result of such incidents. It clearly shows why infantry and crewmen rarely travelled inside an APC, and indicates the hazards faced by drivers. (Private collection)

to each tactical zone, other factors were also significant, and the methods of employment outlined below were not necessarily common throughout Vietnam or even during a particular phase of the war.

To the north in I CTZ, the bulk of the population lived along a 15-mile-wide strip of coastal rice–growing land. 3rd Marine Amphibious Force (III MAF), employing Marine Corps doctrine, tactics and techniques, operated in this area and along the Demilitarized Zone (DMZ) to counter infiltration from North Vietnam and Laos.

The II CTZ was characterised by extreme variations in terrain, with the heavily-populated coastal plains to the east, the rugged belt of the Annamite mountains covering two thirds of the zone and the thickly forested highlands to the west presenting formidable obstacles to mobility. Strong main force NVA units and a primary infiltration route through Laos and Cambodia combined to constitute a significant enemy threat in the area.

The III CTZ containing the major population centre of Saigon, the political heart of the Republic, was flanked by dense mangrove swamps and by gently rolling hills and plains, interspersed with dense jungle growth; it was, however, quite suitable for the employment of AFVs. Hardcore enemy units, predominantly VC, had developed a series of long-established base areas around Saigon together with a deeply entrenched political infrastructure.

In IV CTZ, primarily an ARVN area of operations, a combination of dense population, flat rice paddy terrain, heavy mangrove swamps and the tactics employed by the enemy rendered operations quite

distinct in character from those in the other three CTZs.

The warfare conducted in Vietnam was variously described as 'non-lineal', 'multi-directional', 'unconventional', 'counter-insurgency' or 'area warfare', the latter being the preferred term. 'Area warfare' results when armed forces seeking to achieve control of the population of a country are unable, or do not wish, to conduct military operations in the traditional sense, i.e. by the seizure of a succession of terrain objectives while maintaining a continuous front between one's own forces and the enemy.

US forces' participation in 'area warfare' in Vietnam was characterised by widespread tactical offensive operations by units varying from platoon to multi-divisional size. Combat operations were logistically supported from permanent unit base camps widely located throughout the Republic. The unit base camps in turn were dependent on large logistical installations established in coastal enclaves in the vicinity of deep-water ports. US tactical offensive operations had as their general goal the location and destruction of the enemy armed forces—as distinct from the seizure of terrain objectives—while, concurrently, providing security to their own base camps and supporting logistical installations and the lines of communication between them.

In support of combat operations, armored units undertook a wide variety of missions which may be classified under three headings—'search and destroy', 'clear and secure' and 'security'—embracing all offensive and defensive operations.

'Search and destroy' operations were conducted to locate enemy installations, destroy or evacuate supplies and equipment and to destroy or capture enemy forces. Less importance was attached to seizing and holding critical terrain than finding and destroying the enemy's armed forces and political infrastructure. During a 'search and destroy' mission armor and mechanised infantry units initially engaged in area reconnaissance involving 'movement to contact'. When contact with the enemy occurred they would undertake offensive operations reinforced by air cavalry, artillery, close air support and airmobile or attached infantry—this was known as 'Pile On', a tactic whereby superior forces were amassed at the point of contact. The majority of offensive operations in Vietnam fell into this category, and all armor units participated in 'search and destroy' missions.

'Clear and secure' missions were offensive operations undertaken to drive enemy forces from a designated area and secure it against their return. These operations were generally initiated by 'search and destroy' actions but differed in that they were of longer duration, and emphasised the seizure and holding of key population and communication centres followed by civic action programmes as part of the 'hearts and minds' strategy of 'pacification'.

'Security' operations involved convoy, route, base and area security as well as reaction force missions, all of which were of vital importance in area warfare, since the enemy was liable to attack from any direction at almost any time. Convoy security was accomplished by securing the route to be used or by accompanying the convoy with an appropriate mix of combat units. The time involved was limited to that required to complete the movement of the convoy. By their nature, the others were generally of longer duration and, like 'clear and secure' operations, were conducted with some 'search and destroy' actions. These security operations were for the purpose of clearing and holding roads and installations. They were usually conducted with minimum forces. If attacked, security forces were supported by quick-reaction reserves from nearby bases. Because of their mobility, armor and mechanised infantry units were well suited to security duties and particularly to reaction force missions.

SEARCH AND DESTROY OPERATIONS

A typical 'search and destroy'[1] mission executed by armored and mechanised infantry units was accomplished in three phases: first, isolation of the area by surrounding it with troops or placing elements in blocking positions across likely avenues of enemy escape; second, a mounted sweep through the area with tanks leading, to disrupt any organised resistance, to detonate mines and booby traps and to locate and to destroy all enemy personnel and emplacements; and finally, one or more thorough searches by dismounted personnel accompanied by tanks and APCs.

Most 'search and destroy' operations involved infantry, armor, air, artillery, engineer and other combat support units. Because of the elusive nature of the enemy, and his ability to disengage rather than fight against superior forces, it was of paramount importance to 'fix' the enemy once contact was gained. This was achieved by placing

[1] The term 'search and destroy' superceded 'search and kill', and was superceded in its turn by the blander phase 'reconnaissance in force'.

72

'Deadheaded' behind two M113s acting as ground anchors, an M88 VTR of Troop C, 1/1st Cavalry, employing the correct use of winch and cable with the blade lowered for purchase, frees an M48A3 bogged in muddy terrain during an operation in the Pineapple Forest west of Tam Ky, December 1967. Abuse of the powerful M88 was all too frequent, when crews simply attached tow cables and put 'pedal to the metal' in the hope of extricating stricken vehicles. (Armor Magazine)

supporting fire to the rear and flanks of the enemy to contain his withdrawal, while armored forces led the attack with infantry providing close protection for the vehicles. Those units without armored support were at a grave disadvantage because the close range of the majority of engagements precluded the employment of supporting fire on enemy forces directly in contact unless the unit withdrew. Withdrawal, even for a short distance, resulted in breaking contact and the minimal, but inevitable, delay in supporting fire being brought to bear frequently permitted the enemy to escape. The time lag for fire support was commonly five minutes for artillery, 15 for gunships and 20 for ground-attack aircraft. Although impressive by any standards, this was still long enough to allow the enemy to withdraw—though units with integral air support were often able to cut response time to seconds rather than minutes.

Traditionally, armor has been used as a manoeuvre element while infantry is employed as a holding force, but in area warfare surprise and speed were essential in the deployment of the enveloping force. Airmobile infantry was found to be more effective for this role in Vietnam while, conversely, armor was better suited to executing the supporting attack to 'fix' the enemy, thanks to its inherent protection against hostile fire and its ability in many areas to negotiate jungle and rice paddies at a greater speed than that of infantry.

This reversal of roles extended to operations in the jungle when, for the protection of AFVs from tank-hunter teams, contemporary doctrine stated: 'Infantry normally dismount to lead an attack

73

LEFT

A symphony in brute force: an M88 VTR digs an emplacement for an AFV of Troop B, 3/4th Cavalry during Operation 'Cedar Falls', first of the multi-division combined arms operations of the war, in the Iron Triangle north-west of Saigon, January 1967. The use of the front-mounted blade for engineer tasks such as this was discouraged, as any damage incurred while digging could render the vehicle incapable of performing its primary task of recovery. The armored pulpit around the commander's hatch was a non-standard fitting but gunshields and additional M2 Brownings were common on M88s in Vietnam. (US Army CC38101)

ABOVE RIGHT

A superb study of the M88 in action as two VTRs lift a mine-damaged M48A3 of 'Delta' Co., 11 ACR on to the rear bed of an M123A1C/M15A2 'Dragon Wagon' tank transporter, 1969. The M88 VTR was the workhorse of recovery units in Vietnam, and the success of many armored operations depended on the availability and staying power of these outstanding vehicles and their crews. A complete powerpack change could be achieved in under four hours. (John Graber)

through heavily wooded terrain.' Because of the enemy's use of anti-personnel mines and booby traps and his propensity for mounting ambushes in jungle areas, tanks led the way whenever possible, breaking trails, detonating mines and disrupting enemy defences. Mechanised infantry followed the tanks to complete the destruction of the enemy and to make dismounted sweeps of the area to obtain intelligence and to destroy enemy units and installations.

Throughout the war, accurate and timely intelligence on the location of the enemy proved to be an intractable problem. To a certain extent 'search and destroy' tactics were adopted because units were obliged to conduct operations with little specific knowledge of enemy activity, the aim being to locate him through contact and then destroy him. This meant that engagements were frequently fought only on ground and at times of the enemy's choosing. Nevertheless, once the enemy was brought to battle the shock action and firepower of armored units were invariably decisive, as this vivid account of mounted combat affirms:

1100 hrs, 20 August 1967. The radio in the operations centre crackled into life: 'Cougar six-five, this is Thunderball five-zero-yankee. SITREP no change. We're still moving north about 1,000 metres in from the beach.' 'This is six-five. Roger, out.'

Team Hocker, callsign 'Thunderball', commanded by Capt. Bill Hocker, comprised Company C, 2nd Battalion, 34th Armor, and the reconnaissance platoon of 2nd Battalion, 35th Infantry. Commanded by Lt. Homer Krout, the recon platoon was known as 'Krout's Killers'. The two units had been cross-attached in the field by the CO of the 'Cacti Blue' (2/35th Infantry), Lt. Col. Norman L. Tiller or 'Cougar Six'. They, together with Sgt. Dieter Burger's 'Thunderball five-zero-yankee' made Team Hocker a formidable combination.

'Cougar six-five, this five-zero-yankee. We've got a resupply bird coming in a few minutes and we'll be holding until we get this resupply finished.'

Men of Co. C, 1st Bn.,
5th Infantry
(Mechanized) of 25th
Inf. Div. deploy a
Marginal Terrain
Assault Bridge during
operations in the 'Fish
Hook' area of
Cambodia, May 1970.
An assault bridge
mounted on the M113
APC was designed—
and the first prototype
built —at the US Army
Mobility and
Equipment Research
and Development
Center at Fort Belvoir,
Virginia; 29
production vehicles

'Cougar six-five. OK, but move out on that mission ASAP! Over?'
'Five-zero-yankee. Roger, out.'

The mission was to move to the hamlet of An Tho and conduct a detailed search in order to root out the enemy and destroy his infrastructure, so diminishing his influence in the area.

'Five-zero-yankee, this is Cougar six-five. Dolphin [the 174th Assault Helicopter Company] reports that your resupply bird picked up some ground fire north of your location.'

'This is Thunderball six. What co-ordinates?'

'This is six-five. Vicinity bravo-sierra-eight-zero-zero-four-six-zero, about five minutes ago.'

'Six-five, this is five-zero-yankee. Roger, We'll check it out.'

Capt. Hocker sent a section of three tanks north toward the area of the ground-to-air fire. No sooner had they arrived than the leading tank spotted two enemy soldiers running along a trench and opened fire, killing one. At once all three tanks were raked by automatic weapons fire.

were built by the Unit
Rig and Equipment
Company of Tulsa,
Oklahoma, and 25 were
deployed to Vietnam in
1969. (US Army
SC657033)

RIGHT
*Based on the same
chassis as the M107
and M110 SPGs, the
M578 was designed as
a light recovery vehicle
to support M113 units.
Despite its lack of
amphibious capability
it proved adequate in
this capacity, but with
the introduction of the
M551 into armored
squadrons the M578
was strained to the
limit. Accordingly, the
M578 was not as
successful as its
powerful stablemate,
the M88, but was
extensively employed
for lack of anything
better. The M578 was
known as the
'cherrypicker' from its
similarity in
appearance to the
agricultural equipment
used for fruit picking in
the orchards of southern
California. A heavily-
armed M578 of Troop
I, 11 ACR, mounting
two Brownings, moves
through FSB
Hampton, 1968. Note
the broom wedged
between the gas bottles
of the cutting
equipment, carried by
many AFVs to sweep
away the dreaded red
ants that infested
vehicles when operating
in the jungle. (James
Loop)*

'Six-five, this is five-zero-yankee. Contact! Receiving automatic weapons fire from the north and north-west. How about some Aloha Birds?'
'Six-five. Rog. Got location?'
'Five-zero-yankee. Eight-one-two-five-five, over.'
'Six-five. I gotcha. On the way.'
The remainder of Team Hocker moved north to join the three tanks in the firefight. Meanwhile, the brigade forward air controller, callsign Helix-two-two, was circling the battle in his 'bird-dog'.
'Hello, down there, this is Helix-two-two. What's all the rumpus?'
'Helix, this is five-zero-yankee. We've been getting some automatic weapons fire from the north and north-west of where those three tanks are. How about taking a look?'
'Yankee, Helix here. How about having your tank pop smoke?'
'Rog, Helix. Smoke on the way.'
'Five-zero-yankee, Helix here. I got your smoke. Identify red?'
'Helix, this is five-zero-yankee. That's affirm. North and north-west of that smoke is where the fire is coming from.'
'Rog, Yankee. I'm going down for a look.'
While the 'bird-dog' made an aerial reconnaissance, the H23 observation helicopters of the brigade aviation section were already 'pulling pitch'. With two door gunners, the 'Alohas' were feared by the enemy almost as much as the heavily armed Huey gunships, the 'Sharks'.
Thunderball rolled north and joined its three companions, turning north-west in a full scale attack against the enemy positions now under aerial observation by Helix-two-two, who reported that he saw ten to 20 armed men in the village of An Thach. The tanks deployed on line.

The M548 appeared in several guises: as a cargo carrier, ammunition resupply vehicle and, as shown, a liquid transporter carrying standard ordnance liquid tanks of various types on the cargo bed. This M548 is used as a resupply vehicle to a Land Clearing Team. The M548 proved most useful in operational areas inaccessible to wheeled resupply vehicles. (James Loop)

The enemy fire increased. An M48A3 on the right was hit. Two men were wounded.

'Cougar six-five, this is five-zero-yankee, over.'

'This is six-five, go!'

'This is five-zero-yankee. Got two whiskey-india-alpha. Not bad. Need Dustoff at co-ordinates eight-zero-five-four-six-zero. Over.'

'This is six-five. Roger that. Come up on Dustoff's push. Do you need guns? Over.'

'This is five-zero-yankee. Standby ... Six-five, this is yankee. Affirm on those gunships. Six wants them on the Thunderball freq, over.'

'This is six-five. Roger. Aloha is airborne and will be coming up on your push. Sharks will be out in about five minutes. Over.'

Above the noise of the battle came the characteristic and reassuring *whop, whop, whop* of the heavily laden gunships, taking up orbits around the area. The enemy had the western half of An Thach. Thunderball had the eastern. Suddenly Helix spotted several enemy moving along a trench on the south side of the hamlet. Hocker turned Aloha loose while the Sharks stood by.

'Helix two-two, this is Aloha zero-one, would you mark that trench where you saw the dinks?'

'Roger, Aloha. Turning in for a mark now. Mark, away.'

'Helix, this is zero-one. I got your whiskey-papa just west of that red-roofed hootch.'

'This is Helix. That's affirm.'

'Aloha, zero-seven, this is zero-one. I'm going to make a run down the trench heading west. Cover me on the right.'

'Zero-seven, Roger.'

In late 1968 a test platoon of six XM163 air defence vehicles was deployed to Vietnam for combat trials where they were used mainly for convoy escort. The XM163 was based on a modified chassis of the M113A1, designated XM741, and mounted a Vulcan M16A1 six-barrelled Gatling gun firing at a rate of 1,000 or 3,000 rounds per minute. The 'Vulcan Test Unit' was attached to 5/2nd Arty. operating out of Long Binh. Vehicles 1 and 2 had Range-Only-Radar installed, while vehicles 3 to 6 had dummy radars. (James Loop)

'Shark Lead, this is Aloha zero-one. I've got a bunch in this trench below me. Can you give me a hand?'

'Zero-one, Shark Lead. Roger, I see 'em. Move out of the way. We'll be rolling in from east to west.'

'This is zero-one. I'm clear. Give 'em hell!'

The exploding rockets momentarily drew everyone's attention as the Sharks poured fire on the enemy position. Hocker, realising the enemy were occupying An Thach in force, moved one of his platoons further to the north. Krout's men moved with the tanks to protect them from tank-killer teams. The fight raged on. Thunderball pressed the attack into An Thach. The resistance became fanatical. One Viet Cong charged the lead tank firing his BAR, only to be blasted to smithereens by 90mm gunfire. Overhead in the command and control helicopter, Col. Tiller decided to insert A and B Companies into the battle.

'Thunderball six, this is Cougar six. I'm going to put Alpha in if I can get the lift ships. Where do you want him?'

'Cougar six, this is Thunderball six. It would be best if you put him in on that open field just south of An Thach.'

'This is Cougar six. Roger, out.'

'Five-zero-yankee, this is Cougar six. What's your situation now?'

'This is five-zero-yankee. We're right in the centre of them now. We've been killing them left and right. I don't know how many. They're everywhere. Wait, out!'

Thunderball attacked due west into the centre of An Thach

An M132A1 'Zippo' engages a hedgerow with flame. The M132A1 carried 200 gallons of fuel with a flaming duration of 32 seconds to a range of 150 metres; it was widely known as 'Zippo' after the well-known cigarette lighter, which gained a certain notoriety in Vietnam. Barbed wire coils for night defensive positions were often carried along the sides of APCs, where they swung, leaving characteristic scouring marks down to the bare aluminium. (US Army SC639315)

achieving the classic armor penetration which split the enemy into two forces, one on the north side of the penetration and the other on the south. Aggressively exploiting their success, they pursued the enemy until the VC split into even smaller units, attempting to flee the tanks and APCs. Realising the western escape route was sealed by the low-flying helicopters, the enemy adopted suicidal tactics. Following the lead of their dead BAR man, several charged directly at the command tank, but to no avail.

'Cougar six, this is yankee. Two of 'em just jumped on my track. They're KiA. We're still moving west. I can see the rice paddy ahead. I think they're broken up now.'

'Five-zero-yankee, this is Cougar six. Good. Keep rolling. The paddy on the west is covered by Aloha and the Sharks. They won't slip out of there.'

'This is Thunderball six. Roger that. When we reach the paddy, request permission to reverse course and cover the hamlet again. We didn't get several dinks that darted into holes. Over?'

'This is Cougar six. Permission granted. We'll put Alpha down to the south-east and have them block that corner. Bravo is working

A 'Zippo' is replenished
with fuel for its M10-8
flamethrower from a
mixing unit mounted on
an XM45E1, an
armored version of the
M548 employed in
limited numbers in
Vietnam as a service
vehicle to mechanised
flamethrower units.
The 'Zippo' is
appropriately but grimly
named 'BURN BABY
BURN', and the
XM45E1 'LAVIDA',
Spanish for 'Life'.
(James Loop)

south along the paddies and can cover the northern escape route.
We've got all exits blocked.'

The scheme of manoeuvre directed by the battalion commander in
effect boxed in any enemy who may have been bypassed in
Thunderball's first attack. When Capt. Hocker reached the western
edge of An Thach he turned his tanks around to retrace their tracks.
Thunderball had killed 26 enemy and captured nine weapons
including a 60mm mortar. At the same time Company A completed
the air assault on a landing zone south of An Thach and immediately
began a systematic search of the village. The battle was over.

'Thunderball six, this is Cougar six. Do you have an LZ where I
can land and talk?'

'This is Thunderball six. Rog. We'll secure one next to our
PC. Standby for smoke.'

'This is Cougar six. Roger, I have your violet smoke. On the way
in.'

That day, An Thach yielded 53 enemy dead and 18 weapons. The
official report of the action states:

'Captain Hocker repeatedly concentrated his forces in overwhelming strength at the enemy's location as reported by aerial observers.
This outstanding employment of tanks and infantry together with the
firepower and manoeuver of the tanks and the close-in fighting of the
infantry, resulted in the virtual annihilation of the 2nd Company,
97th Battalion, 2nd VC Regiment.'

LINES OF COMMUNICATION SECURITY
One of the major tasks of US and Allied forces in South Vietnam was
to provide secure ground routes for both military and commercial
traffic. The security of lines of communication and supply has been a
traditional mission for armored units. Tank and mechanised infantry
units were suited to this task, but armored cavalry units were judged
superior. On many occasions the limited Allied capability for aerial
resupply of isolated positions made this a vital mission, and armored
units spent approximately one-third of their time on this duty.

The enemy's aims in denying free use of the roads was the

One of the most
spectacular recovery
techniques devised in
Vietnam employed the
redoubtable CH-47
Chinook Medium Lift
Helicopter to retrieve
M113 APCs bogged
down in paddy fields.
Even APCs mired to
their hulltops could be
extracted by the more
powerful CH-54 Sky
Crane. This M113 of
3/4th Cavalry has the
early Okinawa pattern
hatch armor for the
commander. (US
Army SC651997)

collection of 'taxes' from civilian traffic, and the setting of ambushes for allied troops. Route security required the continuous commitment of large forces over long periods, and included the protection of key points such as bridges. On major routes these were normally guarded by RF/PF units from local areas. In the absence of such forces, outposts (known as 'thunders') were established along the road and mobile patrols operated between them.

As some units moved supply convoys at night, to avoid interfering with civilian traffic, it was necessary to provide secure routes on a continuous basis. At night the outposts scattered along the route, consisting of a few vehicles and an infantry squad, were vulnerable to attack, so continuous patrols known as 'thunder runs' were maintained. A run involved AFVs moving in column with tanks in the van and other vehicles at close intervals, moving at high speed and undertaking 'reconnaissance by fire' along the roadsides to trigger potential ambushes. While this tactic increased vehicle mileage and hence maintenance problems, it did serve to discourage enemy mining of roads. As in all operations in Vietnam, it was essential to avoid establishing a pattern while 'thunder running'.

Another technique, known as 'road running' after the cartoon character, was undertaken by AFVs travelling a road for the purpose of keeping the enemy off balance, and for making the presence of friendly forces felt among the local populace. 'Road runs' took place both by day and by night.

CONVOY ESCORT

The numerous logistic bases necessary for Allied operations throughout the Republic highlighted the importance of route security and convoy escort operations. The continuous, relatively uninterrupted movement of convoys over land lines of communication was essential to the military effort as well as to the stability of the country. Road networks that were sufficiently secure for military traffic were used by commercial enterprises, thereby

improving the economic situation and the degree of government control of the area through which the road passed. The enemy was well aware of the effect free road movement had on his efforts to control the population, and a major part of his forces was assigned to interdict roads.

Military Police units have traditionally undertaken convoy escort duties. In Vietnam they were too few in number and, until issued with the V-100 Commando armored car in 1968, inadequately equipped to counter the ferocity of enemy ambush techniques that had been perfected over 20 years. In consequence, the task of convoy escort fell to armored units whose mobility, flexible communications and concentrated firepower proved a potent deterrent to ambush.

Armored vehicles were assigned to escort convoys in the ratio of one per five to ten supply trucks. The configuration of the convoy naturally depended on the terrain, the number of vehicles and the estimated enemy threat. The two leading vehicles were often tanks, as they provided maximum firepower to the front and were capable of clearing any obstacles on the road, including pressure-detonated mines. The balance of the escort was spaced throughout the convoy and another tank took up the rear with its turrent facing aft.

As there were insufficient armored or Military Police units to protect all the convoys plying the roads of Vietnam, transportation units devised the expedient of 'hardening' some cargo vehicles. The beds of 2½- and 5-ton trucks were floored with armor plate or sandbags, and side and front protection was fitted. Some vehicles were configured as 'gun trucks' and armed with M60 and .50 cal. machine guns as surrogate AFVs. Convoy control jeeps were also armored, as were other 'softskin' transports impressed as escorts for 'line-haul' operations. By these expedients transportation units were able to provide a measure of their own security, albeit at the cost of a loss of carrying capability, and the assignment of one tenth of their manpower to an infantry role.

AMBUSH AND COUNTER-AMBUSH

The principal military strategy of the NVA and VC was to retain the initiative through continuous offensive action. They tended to favour three basic tactical operations: the raid, the ambush, and the attack by fire. Their aim was to inflict maximum casualties and to destroy equipment and installations. Against armor-supported formations the most common form of attack was the ambush.

A typical ambush was planned to capitalise on surprise by delivering an initially large volume of fire in order to immobilise and disorganise a unit in the first seconds, followed by rapid withdrawal before reaction forces were committed. Normally, the enemy did not ambush a pure armored formation unless he was well prepared in a fortified position with an abundance of anti-tank weapons. Enemy emplacements were well camouflaged to avoid detection and were established in depth to enable withdrawal under fire. Such positions were often selected in areas that did not lend themselves to immediate counter-attack by mounted forces, due either to the type of vegetation—such as bamboo thickets—or the inability of the ground to support armor.

It was not uncommon for enemy forces to be dispersed over an area that presented a 'killing zone' in excess of one kilometre. The usual technique was to blow up the lead vehicle with a command-detonated mine; another was then detonated among the rearguard to obstruct retreat. The roadsides were often mined and the ditches lined with punji-stakes and booby traps to inflict casualties among personnel dismounting to seek cover. The whole ambush area would be covered by mortars, recoilless rifles and automatic weapons. In many instances, secondary ambushes were laid for the reaction forces. After a short and violent attack, with the emphasis on inflicting casualties, the ambushers would make a rapid withdrawal.

All cavalry units in Vietnam devised their own standard operating procedures (SOP) for counter-ambush tactics, with basic techniques, developed from past experience, modified to meet the particular situation and terrain. The key to defeating an ambush was rapid, aggressive, rehearsed response. When an ambush was sprung reactions were, to say the least, elemental. Drivers did not stop, as this created stationary targets. Unarmored vehicles continued out of the 'killing zone', pushing disabled vehicles aside. AFVs left the road when possible, and assaulted the enemy. Forward elements, which had already passed the ambush, 'clover-leafed' around the enemy and

Carrying men of 1st Bn., 28th Infantry Regt. of 1st Inf. Div., 'BATMAN' leads a column of M48A3s of 1st Sqn., 4th Cavalry ('Quarterhorse'), through the jungle of War Zone C during Operation 'Junction City', March 1967. This was the largest operation of the war up to that date, with combined arms operations at battalion and squadron level. Armored task forces, with attached elements of infantry and artillery, roamed through the operational area. Tanks were invaluable in breaking trails across seemingly impenetrable terrain. (US Army SC639790)

The numerous watercourses and the soft marshy ground in many areas of Vietnam were constant impediments to tank movements. This M48A3 of Troop A, 1/1st Cavalry, hopelessly 'bellied-up' in mud in August 1968, typifies the problem. The G305 turret cupola vision riser was fitted to final production 'A3' Pattons, designated M48A3 (Late Model). This device appeared in Vietnam during mid-1967 and was intended to provide the tank commander with improved all-round vision under armor, but as few 'TCs' ever travelled or fought 'buttoned-up', it proved of limited value. (US Army CC50585)

M48A3 tanks of 2/34th Armor slew into herringbone formation after receiving fire during an operation in Binh Long Province. Deployed in this manner, the tanks deliver a high volume of fire over a wide area to counter ambushes from roadsides. (US Army SC636351)

charged his flanks. Throughout these actions every AFV laid down a heavy volume of fire in assigned sectors.

One of the most widespread counter-measures was the 'herringbone formation'. This was developed by 1st Squadron, 4th Cavalry, the first armored cavalry unit to be deployed to Vietnam, and was subsequently adopted by many others. It was employed when forward movement of an armored column or convoy had been stopped by an ambush covering a section of the route from which vehicles could not deploy. The aim was to direct all available firepower on the suspected enemy position. SOP required all AFVs to stop, to pivot at an angle with alternate vehicles facing to either side of the road, and to fire all weapons. AFVs closed rapidly to within a few yards of each other to achieve an even higher density of firepower. If terrain permitted, most armored units moved to close with and kill the enemy instead of assuming this formation. This technique was also employed by armored units to leapfrog along a line of march in dangerous areas. The first platoon halted in the herringbone formation; the second platoon passed through the first and assumed the same pattern, the process being repeated until the suspicious area had been crossed.

RIGHT
In the aftermath of the 1968 Tet offensive heavy tank losses dictated the deployment of the M48A2C model as replacements. Being gasoline powered, the 'A2 Charlie' was less popular with crews because of its reduced range and greater fire risk. Here 'A2s' and ACAVs of 4th Sqn., 12th Cavalry, deploy beside Highway 1 as a reaction force, August 1968. The engineer stakes at each corner of the nearer ACAVs acted as supports for a sunshield. (US Army CC51322)

BELOW LEFT
'Reconnaissance by fire'—an M48A3 of Co. C, 1/69th Armor fires main armament and .50 cal. rounds into likely ambush sites to clear the way for a convoy to pass along Highway 14 west of An Khe, June 1969. (US Army SC650950)

OPPOSITE BELOW
'Loaded for bear'—the TC of a heavily-laden M48A3 of Co. C ('Fighting Aces') 2/34th Armor engages a VC sniper's position with his 'fifty'. To the crews, the tanks were their homes, and they were festooned with all manner of creature comforts as well as the tools of war—C-ration cartons, folding cots, minigun boxes, spare trackblocks, roadwheels et al—anything that increased firepower, protection and self-sufficiency. Tanks were commonly given names, often outrageous or scatalogical in nature, written along the gun barrel or bore evacuator. This M48A3 is called 90 PROOF. (Armor Magazine)

OPPOSITE

Deep in 'Indian Country' near the Rock Pile, a fire support base in Military Region I, an M48A3 (Late Model) of Co. C, 1st Bn., 77th Armor sets up a night defensive position behind a length of cyclone fencing attached to engineer stakes, March 1971. The chain-link screen was erected whenever AFVs halted for any length of time—and always at night. It served to protect vehicles against rocket attack by detonating RPG rounds before they hit the target. (US Army SC660516)

OPPOSITE BELOW

Forging through dense undergrowth, an M48A3 of 1st Sqn., 10th Cavalry patrols the bush alongside Highway 19 near An Khe, February 1971. For most of its five years in Vietnam 1/10th Cavalry repetitiously secured the road network in the Pleiku area of IICTZ. The M2 Browning is welded forward of the loader's hatch on an M113 APC mount for use by the gunner. In the heat of the tropics the gunner rarely rode at his position in the turret, where it was commonly 20° above the ambient temperature, frequently rising above 120°F. The loader remained inside the turret only when in contact, to serve the 90mm gun which the commander laid and fired from his M1 cupola. (US Army SC660326)

SECURITY PERIMETER DEFENCE

While the emphasis of armor employment was primarily on offensive operations, some of the largest 'kills' of the war occurred when the enemy tried to overrun defensive positions. In general, armored units did not 'defend ground' in the sense of past wars, but instead assumed a defensive posture when not actively engaged in offensive operations. At times armored units of all sizes were assigned static perimeter defence missions, for the security of either a permanent base camp, headquarters elements, a fire support base or a forward combat base. Although mobility and shock action were compromised in such circumstances, the use of armored units in this role was valid, particularly during the wet season, as it freed other forces for operations in terrain unsuited to armor.

Invariably, enemy attacks on base areas were preceded by artillery, mortar or rocket barrages. The digging-in of vehicles and the construction of foxholes or bunkers was therefore necessary, as the majority of casualties among armor personnel were inflicted by the first incoming rounds while crewmen moved to mount vehicles. Each vehicle was protected by an earth berm, sandbags, or an 'RPG screen' of cyclone fencing as stand-off protection from anti-tank weapons. Such protective measures were also employed in 'laager' positions—a defensive formation adopted by combat units whenever they halted for extended periods, usually at night. Thanks to the enemy's lack of tactical air capability and his limited artillery, it was possible to establish laager positions in open terrain with the vehicles positioned close together. The primary consideration was mutual support in the event of a mass attack or sapper infiltration.

As a disincentive to enemy action, armored units customarily indulged in a 'mad minute' soon after nightfall when all weapons fired at maximum rate from all points of the perimeter for a set time. The overwhelming volume of fire from an armored unit often discouraged further enemy activity. When they did attack such positions, enemy units did so at their peril, as this graphic account by Sergeant Robert Lagana testifies:

Our troop was busy setting up a night laager position outside a large village close to the base of Nui Ba Dinh (Black Virgin Mountain) in Tay Ninh Province on 18 June 1969. Earlier in the evening, trip flares had been positioned 80 to 100 metres to the front of all the vehicles, each crew careful to overlap theirs with the next to ensure an unbroken early-warning line against the hardcore VC working the area. RPG screens had been erected in front of all the 113s and Sheridan tanks, fighting holes dug, and claymore mines positioned.

The men on Track 12[1] and I began to relax and talk about our day's fruitless sweep of the jungle around the base of the Black Virgin. Darkness and the promise of rain kept the crews of the 113s close to their vehicles. Tonight we wouldn't socialise with the other crews over a warm beer, since the inky-black tropical night made even the Starlight scopes ineffective. Hours limped by.

Suddenly, the horizon blazed with light. Two trip flares were burning brightly 100 metres north of the laager. As if on cue, trip flares went off all around our encampment.

[1] 'Track'—universal nickname for the M113, and by extension for any tracked AFV in Vietnam.

OPPOSITE
The majority of rounds fired by tanks in Vietnam were canister or 'Beehive', reflecting the close range of most engagements. 'Beehive' superseded canister, as it had a variable time fuse with settings for detonation from point-blank range out to 4,000 metres. A canister round contained 1,280 segments and was similar in action to a gigantic shotgun shell, spreading a swathe of metal shards from the gun muzzle to a distance of 250 metres. It proved highly effective in stripping vegetation concealing enemy positions, and equally so against obstacles such as barbed wire entanglements, or even to detonate mines in the path of a tank—a technique employed in areas where mines were likely.

The 'Beehive' round contained 5,000 to 10,000 'flechettes' (or darts), depending on the calibre; these were deadly against enemy personnel. These photographs graphically illustrate the effect of canister on jungle growth and an enemy slit trench which moments before had been covered by undergrowth. The extensive use of canister led to the cracking of blast deflectors on M48A3s after the firing of 100 rounds or so—a rate far beyond the design parameters of the 90mm gun. (Private collection)

ABOVE
'Bunker-busting'—the 52 tons of an M48A3 (Late Model) of 2/34th Armor make short work of an enemy bunker system near Cu Chi, February 1969. Once detected, enemy positions were invariably destroyed to prevent further use—either by explosives or, just as effectively, by being crushed under the tracks of tanks. (Armor Magazine)

C Troop opened up with .50 cals., M60s and Sheridan main guns. The tanks facing the village held their fire, even though trip flares were going off directly in front of them. I heard my driver, Sol, scrambling beneath the commander's hatch toward his driver's seat. My two gunners were behind their M60s, laying down perfectly timed bursts. My .50 cal. shook the 113. Tracers arched into the night, and adrenalin pumped through tired bodies.

After what seemed like hours, I heard the Old Man through my CVC helmet: 'Cease fire! Cease fire!' The guns stuttered to a halt. Complete and utter silence. Nothing moved. Tension lay as thick as the tropical night.

Bursts of .50 cal. at real or imagined sounds and movement punctuated the rest of the night. Nerves on edge, 100 per cent alert, no one slept. What was going on? We heard no return fire, not one round.

The sun rose red as a malignant eye, slowly focusing on us. Because we'd expended so much ammo in the 'recon by fire', the Old Man arranged for a resupply convoy to link up with us. Tracks 11 and 12 were to proceed one kilometre to the village on the hardtop road to receive the resupply. Track 13 pulled an empty 'water buffalo' to exchange for a full one. The three tracks started their engines and struck out on a bearing that would intersect the road south of the village.

We were all on edge. I rechecked the .50 cal., glanced around and saw my gunners going over their weapons—no need for words. We knew our jobs and our tools. Everyone knew something was wrong.

No villagers—no one. Usually they'd be making their way to the fields or to the big market in Tay Ninh. Tracks 11 and 12 covered the kilometre to the road in minutes. It was eerie—no villagers, no movement.

The commander of Track 13 deviated from our predetermined bearing *engineer stakes for the 'RPG screen' lie along the side of the stowage bins; spare track blocks around the turret act as protection against RPGs, with the upper blocks folded over as a stowage shelf for crew kitbags and folding cots; an M60 mounted behind an ACAV gunshield has been welded forward of the loader's hatch; the .50 cal. is mounted above the commander's cupola, with a typist's chair fixed to its hatch and a minigun ammunition box to its side; smoke grenades and machetes are draped around the cupola; a further stowage rack, again fabricated from engineer stakes, has been placed over the engine decks—all combined to make the dependable M48A3 into a formidable fighting machine. (US Army SC654446)*

and broke out of the jungle 200 metres north of our position. As he gained the road we saw a puff of smoke and heard the first RPG slam into the empty 'water buffalo'. The second burst on the flat side of the track, tossing men from its deck onto the ground; I saw my friends scrambling to the ditch by the roadside. Without orders, my driver swung our track around to give the .50 cal. maximum opportunity.

I signalled 11's track commander to cross the road and lay down an intense covering fire in the direction of the disabled 13. Then I looked at Sol and my two gunners. I said, 'Let's get 'em out of there.'

Sol dodged and wove the track. We were in the killzone in what seemed like seconds. My .50 cal. thundered long bursts that ripped up the countryside and kept the VC in their holes, and the blasts of the two M60s alternated with my fire—each man timing his shots so as to reload when the other two gunners were firing. I thought, 'God, don't let us all stop to reload at once.' He was listening.

The men in the ditch dashed for my track and scrambled on. By a miracle no one was killed. AK fire broke my radio antenna. We had lots of holes in the track but none in us. One man from 13 was slightly wounded but not badly enough to keep him from humping .50 cal. ammo for me, grinning and thumping me and my crew on the back.

Suddenly, explosion after explosion nearly tore our shirts off. To my right and left, C Troop was on line, 'kickin' ass and takin' names'—a most welcome sight.

We later learned we had routed a large VC force fortified with NVA. Their intent was to claim control of a large village in III Corps in order to gain concessions at the Paris peace talks. Guess we ruined their plans.

(For his heroism during this ambush. Sgt. Lagana was awarded the Bronze Star.)

One modification to increase the firepower of the M48A3 to the front without exposure of crew members was the substitution of the gunner's M105C telescopic sight for a .50 cal. M2HB Browning. The machine gun is readily apparent protruding from the gun mantlet of this M48A3 of 11 ACR, indicative of the weapon's 61in. length having to be accommodated within the available turret space. This was not a common modification, because at the short ranges of most engagements the standard 7.62mm M73 co-axial machine gun was more than adequate. (John Graber)

RIGHT
The M48A3 tankdozers assigned to tank battalions on an issue of one per company were employed for numerous tasks in support of armored operations. Their roles ranged from cutting paths through jungle for the advance of infantry to ploughing through booby-trapped perimeters of enemy base camps, and from excavating or destroying bunker systems to digging emplacements for tanks and vehicles. Indeed, they performed many of the tasks normally undertaken by combat engineers by virtue of their dedicated attachment to tank battalions. 'Hot Stuff', an M48A3 tankdozer of 11 ACR, mounts an E8 CS gas dispenser above the Xenon searchlight; this projected CS grenades to counter ambushes and close attacks by RPG teams—an effective

MINE WARFARE
Mines were the primary threat to AFVs in Vietnam, causing over 70 per cent of vehicle losses and 20 per cent of casualties. As armored and mechanised units were deployed in greater numbers, the enemy increased his use of anti-vehicle mines; however, he did not employ them in a standard pattern and minefields were, for all intents and purposes, non-existent. The nature of the terrain and enemy tactics did not lend themselves to such traditional thinking; instead the VC employed nuisance mining by scattering mines seemingly at random but on a massive scale.

Anti-tank mines were usually incorporated in ambushes and in the organised defences of base camps and other important installations. They were also employed in large numbers to harass and interdict supply routes, and near combat bases. The majority of mines were of the 'passive' type, detonated by the victim either by the weight of the vehicle passing over a direct pressure plate or by the tilting of a rod protruding upward from the mine. A great many mines, however, were command-detonated. This allowed the enemy to wait in a concealed position and detonate the mine under the vehicle of his choice, usually a priority target such as a command vehicle.

The tactics employed by the enemy were cunning and extremely effective. Two or more mines were often placed in each selected location, which often resulted in additional casualties among personnel moving to assist those wounded by the initial detonation.

Only two variants of
the M60 Main Battle
Tank served in
Vietnam: the M728
CEV, and the M60
AVLB illustrated
here. The 60-foot span
of the folding scissors
bridge was essential to
maintain mobility
across the many
obstacles encountered in
Vietnam. Many
armored operations,
notably the incursions
into Cambodia and
Laos, would have been
impossible without the
AVLB. (US Army
SC650962)

OPPOSITE
Designed to undertake
engineer tasks on the
battlefield, the M728
Combat Engineer
Vehicle (CEV) served
in Vietnam with

Not only did mines and booby traps cause constant casualties;
equally significant was the psychological effect on Allied troops who,
virtually every day, had to clear large portions of the country's road
network. Day in, day out, the steady toll of vehicles and men had a
cumulative effect on the morale on all but the most highly motivated
units, and the troops often had no opportunity to strike back at the
enemy for weeks on end. As an indication of the attrition rate, in June
1966 1st Battalion, 5th Infantry (Mechanized) of 25th Infantry
Division lost 14 M113s to mines in eight days of operations; only
eight of these eventually returned to service. In the period January to
March 1967, on Highway 19 east of Pleiku, 1st Battalion, 69th Armor
found 115 mines; 27 were detected and disarmed, and 88 exploded
with damage to tanks

In most cases, tank hulls proved capable of absorbing the blast of a
mine explosion without serious injuries to the crews or damage to
interior components. As might be supposed, mine damage to APCs
was markedly greater; a correspondingly higher proportion were
designated total losses, particularly among those which were
gasoline-powered. In many cases several crew members were
seriously wounded or killed. Drivers were especially vulnerable and
it was common practice for crew members to rotate this dangerous
job. Troops rarely travelled inside an APC when the threat of mines
was real. Anti-tank mines invariably caused fatalities and serious
damage to equipment inside the stricken vehicle, but commanders
and personnel riding on top often escaped injury.

Several methods were tried in order to increase driver protection.
The most ambitious was to weld extensions to the primary controls

and laterals so that the vehicle could be driven with the driver seated on top, albeit to the detriment of the commander's field of fire. As increased protection against fragments within the vehicle the driving compartment was lined with discarded 'flak jackets'. Sandbags were placed on the floor as additional protection against mines, while some crews removed the driver's seat entirely and substituted a pile of sandbags. Later on, a supplementary 'belly armor' kit was developed and fitted to the hulls of M113s, giving greater protection from mine blast. In the six-month period from November 1968 to May 1969, 73 per cent of all tank and 77 per cent of APC losses were caused by mines. A study conducted in December 1970 revealed that mines still accounted for over 75 per cent of all combat vehicles lost. To overcome the problem, Allied forces attempted to prevent the enemy from laying mines by ambush patrols, sensor-activated artillery fire and the route security techniques of 'thunder runs' and 'road runner' operations. Despite such efforts, the enemy was not prevented from laying mines, so the extravagant toll of AFVs continued.

As early as 1966 field commanders sought better ways of coping with mines. An expendable mine roller was developed under the ENSURE programme at Fort Belvoir, Virginia.[1] The mechanism was mounted in front of an M48A3. The first roller was evaluated in Vietnam during autumn 1969; eventually, 27 were used in Vietnam. It was never fully accepted for, like most of the roller devices used in Vietnam and in earlier wars, the problem lay in surviving the mine it had detonated.

[1] 'ENSURE'— Expediting Non-Standard Urgent Requirements for Equipment.

Tactical Organisation and Equipment

In general, armored units in Vietnam were organised in the same way as those elsewhere in the world. However, local changes were made to meet the demands of different regions within the theatre of operations. Within a short time, no two units in Vietnam were organised or equipped in exactly the same way. The Department of the Army decided that it was impractical to support such a diverse force structure, and enforced strict conformity to tables of organisation and equipment based on recommendations of the MACOV study. The following tables indicate significant organisational changes of the major types of armored units in Vietnam, and equipment changes in regard to AFVs.

TANK UNITS IN VIETNAM
Company D, 16th Armor (173rd Airborne Brigade). May 1965–October 1969. M56 SPAT Scorpion.
2nd Battalion, 34th Armor (25th Infantry Division). Originally assigned to and deployed with 4th Infantry Division, attached to 25th Infantry Division. September 1966–October 1970. M48A3.
1st Battalion, 69th Armor (4th Infantry Division). Originally assigned to and deployed with 25th Infantry Division; attached to 4th Infantry Division. January 1966–April 1970. M48A3.
1st Battalion, 77th Armor (1st Brigade, 5th Infantry Division—Mechanized). July 1968–July 1971. M48A3.

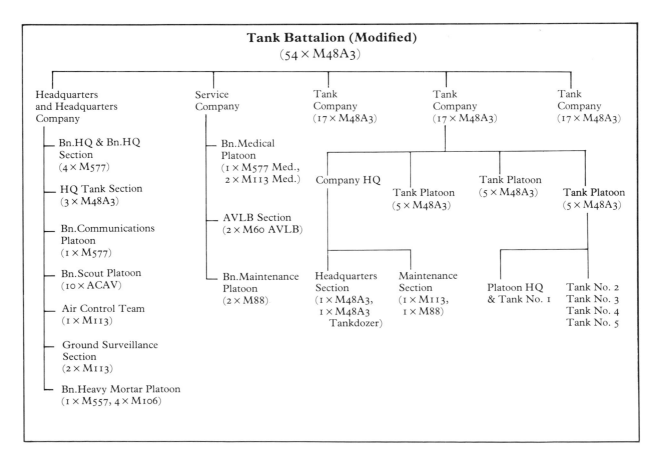

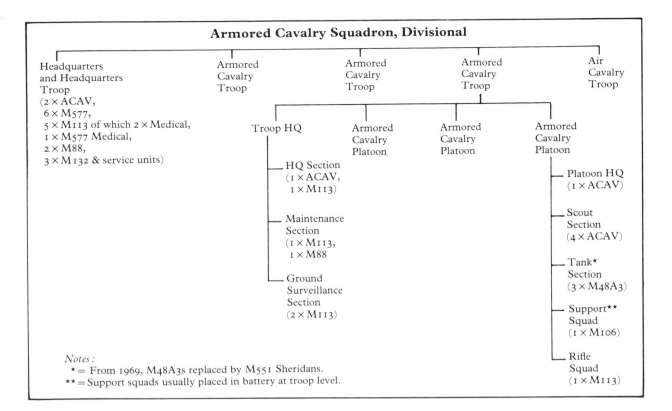

Armored Cavalry Squadron, Divisional

Headquarters and Headquarters Troop
(2 × ACAV,
6 × M577,
5 × M113 of which 2 × Medical,
1 × M577 Medical,
2 × M88,
3 × M132 & service units)

Armored Cavalry Troop

Armored Cavalry Troop

Armored Cavalry Troop

Air Cavalry Troop

Troop HQ

Armored Cavalry Platoon

Armored Cavalry Platoon

Armored Cavalry Platoon

HQ Section
(1 × ACAV,
1 × M113)

Maintenance Section
(1 × M113,
1 × M88)

Ground Surveillance Section
(2 × M113)

Platoon HQ
(1 × ACAV)

Scout Section
(4 × ACAV)

Tank* Section
(3 × M48A3)

Support** Squad
(1 × M106)

Rifle Squad
(1 × M113)

Notes:
  * = From 1969, M48A3s replaced by M551 Sheridans.
  ** = Support squads usually placed in battery at troop level.

GROUND CAVALRY UNITS IN VIETNAM

1st Squadron, 1st Cavalry (23rd Infantry Division—'American'). August 1967–Arpil 1972.

Troop E, 1st Cavalry (11th Infantry Brigade, 23rd Infantry Division). October 1967–October 1971.

2nd Squadron, 1st Cavalry (4th Infantry Division—'Ivy'). August 1967–October 1970.

1st Squadron, 4th Cavalry (1st Infantry Division—'Big Red One'). October 1965–April 1970.

3rd Squadron, 4th Cavalry (25th Infantry Division—'Tropic Lightning'). February 1966–October 1970.

3rd Squadron, 5th Cavalry (9th Infantry Division—'The Old Reliables'). January 1967–October 1971.

1st Squadron, 10th Cavalry (4th Infantry Division). September 1966–November 1971.

Troop A, 4th Squadron, 12th Cavalry (1st Brigade, 5th Infantry Division—Mechanized). July 1968–October 1971.

Troop B, 1st Squadron, 17th Cavalry (82nd Airborne Division). February 1968–February 1970.

2nd Squadron, 17th Cavalry (101st Airborne Division). December 1967–December 1968.

Troop A, 2nd Squadron, 17th Cavalry (101st Airborne Division). July 1965–December 1967.

Troop D, 17th Cavalry (199th Infantry Brigade (Light). December 1966–October 1970.

Troop E, 17th Cavalry (173rd Airborne Brigade). May 1965–August 1971.

Troop F, 17th Cavalry (196th Infantry Brigade, 23rd Infantry Division). September 1965–April 1972.

Troop H, 17th Cavalry (198th Infantry Brigade, 23rd Infantry Division). October 1967–October 1971.

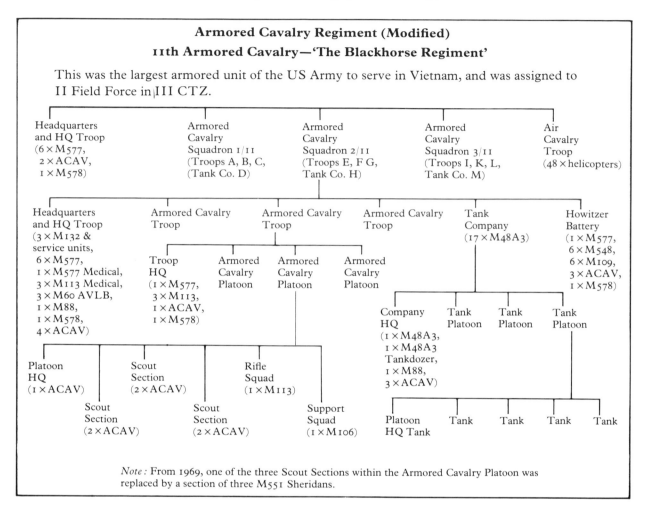

Armored Cavalry Regiment (Modified)
11th Armored Cavalry—'The Blackhorse Regiment'

This was the largest armored unit of the US Army to serve in Vietnam, and was assigned to II Field Force in III CTZ.

Headquarters and HQ Troop (6 × M577, 2 × ACAV, 1 × M578)

Armored Cavalry Squadron 1/11 (Troops A, B, C, (Tank Co. D)

Armored Cavalry Squadron 2/11 (Troops E, F G, Tank Co. H)

Armored Cavalry Squadron 3/11 (Troops I, K, L, Tank Co. M)

Air Cavalry Troop (48 × helicopters)

Headquarters and HQ Troop (3 × M132 & service units, 6 × M577, 1 × M577 Medical, 3 × M113 Medical, 3 × M60 AVLB, 1 × M88, 1 × M578, 4 × ACAV)

Armored Cavalry Troop

Armored Cavalry Troop

Armored Cavalry Troop

Tank Company (17 × M48A3)

Howitzer Battery (1 × M577, 6 × M548, 6 × M109, 3 × ACAV, 1 × M578)

Troop HQ (1 × M577, 3 × M113, 1 × ACAV, 1 × M578)

Armored Cavalry Platoon

Armored Cavalry Platoon

Armored Cavalry Platoon

Company HQ (1 × M48A3, 1 × M48A3 Tankdozer, 1 × M88, 3 × ACAV)

Tank Platoon

Tank Platoon

Tank Platoon

Platoon HQ (1 × ACAV)

Scout Section (2 × ACAV)

Rifle Squad (1 × M113)

Scout Section (2 × ACAV)

Scout Section (2 × ACAV)

Support Squad (1 × M106)

Platoon HQ Tank

Tank

Tank

Tank

Tank

Note: From 1969, one of the three Scout Sections within the Armored Cavalry Platoon was replaced by a section of three M551 Sheridans.

Principal AFVs of the Vietnam War

MI13 ACAV

Undoubtedly the most significant innovation in the employment of armor in Vietnam was the use of the M113 as a fighting vehicle. The M113 had been designed as an armored personnel carrier from which infantry would dismount to fight. The experience of ARVN cavalry units demonstrated that in the terrain, against the particular enemy faced in Vietnam, it was capable of operating in a tank-like role. The Vietnamese developed the concept of mounted combat, and to increase the vehicle's firepower and protection added side-mounted machine guns and armor around the .50 cal. gunner's position. This concept met with considerable resistance from MACV who, even as the first US formations were landing in Vietnam during 1965, were trying to dissuade the Vietnamese from such unorthodox employment. American units quickly adopted the idea, however, and fabricated gunshields from whatever materials were to hand until a standardised version, manufactured in Okinawa, was introduced.

When 11th Armored Cavalry Regiment was preparing for deployment to Vietnam in 1966, it was decided to replace the tanks in the armored cavalry platoons with M113s. These were modified by fitting an armament sub-system designed and manufactured by the FMC Corporation. The 'A Model' kit comprised hatch armor and gunshield for the .50 cal., two M60 machine guns, two elbow pintle

mounts with gunshields for the M60s on each side of the M113, and a removable pintle mount to the rear in which either of the M60s could be positioned. A 'B Model' kit, consisting of hatch armor and gunshield for the commander's .50 cal. only, was produced for mortar carriers, but it was common for such vehicles to have side-mounted M60s as well. With these modifications, the M113 was called the 'Armored Cavalry Assault Vehicle' or ACAV, a term that originated in 1st Squadron, 11 ACR. The ACAV concept soon spread through all US Army units in Vietnam, and the FMC armament system was procured to modify most M113s in theatre.

The ACAV was manned by five or six crew members, depending on unit SOP and manpower, comprising driver, vehicle commander .50 cal. gunner, two M60 gunners and one or two ammunition bearers. The second ammunition bearer also acted as a grenadier with an M79 40mm grenade launcher. Some units demanded that the vehicle commander ride in the rear compartment, as was standard practice in ARVN cavalry regiments, rather than at the .50 cal. machine gun; both configurations had their advocates and both proved effective in combat.

Although the ACAV's standard three-gun battery offered a large volume of fire, there were many modifications to increase offensive firepower. The variety of weapon installations included an automatic 40mm grenade launcher, or alternatively a 7.62mm 'minigun', in place of the .50 cal. Browning; 75mm, 90mm or 106mm recoilless rifles were also mounted atop carriers. Some ACAVs tried .50 cal. guns in place of the side-mounted M60s, although in this configuration the vibration of three heavy machine guns firing at once proved too much for the carrier, fracturing gun mounts and warping the hull. 'Claymorettes' were mounted along the sides to counter ambushes—this was a diminutive version of the M18A1 Claymore anti-personnel mine, which could not itself be used for the purpose as its power would blow a hole in the side of an M113. CS gas dispensers were strapped to the front-mounted trim vanes; and on occasions an

M60 was mounted forward of the driver's position to enable him to fire forwards and downwards into bunkers and trenches.

Besides the diversity of weapons installed, several passive measures were undertaken to bolster the M113's armor protection. At first track shrouds, ammunition boxes, sandbags and spare track blocks were hung over the sides of vehicles, but these were soon torn off when operating in jungle. In early 1966 'bar armor' in the form of spaced steel bars was mounted on the front and sides. These were hinged for folding flat when width was critical; but the system proved unsuitable for several reasons. The mounting bolts tended to strip from the aluminium armor. Crews often found it impractical to dismount in order to retract the 'bar armor' to prevent it being brushed off by trees or the trusses of the narrow French 'Eiffel' bridges. The extra weight also inpaired swimming capability. Other forms of improvised armor included airfield matting, spaced armor or Pierced Steel Planking (PSP). All were intended to detonate the warhead of a shaped charge weapon away from the hull, thus nullifying its power of penetration.

The greatest threat to the M113 remained the landmine, and crews devised several expedient measures to mitigate its effect. In ACAVs, most units laid two layers of ammunition boxes over the sandbags lining the floor. The precautions could be overdone, however; 1st Squadron, 1st Cavalry, who placed two layers of sandbags in all their 'tracks' in addition to all their other equipment and ammunition, suffered 14 transmission breakdowns due to overloading within 45 days. Early in 1967 Army Material Command began development of a mine protection kit comprising titanium armor plates for the hull bottom and sponsons, rerouted fuel lines, and non-integral fuel tanks. By mid-March 1969 US Army Vietnam had tested the first 'belly armor', and it was enthusiastically accepted by crews. As a further measure to protect against mine damage and RPG penetration it was decided in August 1967 to convert the M113 fleet from gasoline to diesel power in order to reduce the danger of fire. At that time 73 per cent of M113s in US Army units in Vietnam were gasoline-powered. By 1 July 1968 the entire APC fleet in US Army Vietnam was equipped with diesel engines. Those powered by diesel engines were designated M113A1.

Effective as 'belly armor' was against mines, the increased weight adversely affected the amphibious capability of the M113. To overcome the problem styrofoam floatation kits were fixed to the front plate and trim vane. Introduced in 1969, these kits proved highly successful except in the Delta, where the added weight of armor and pods caused APCs to bog down in the soft mud. Even in the Delta, however, 'belly armor' and floatation pods were mounted, since the latter gave an unexpected bonus in protection against RPGs.

Throughout the war, the M113 APC and its versatile family of derivatives was enormously effective. In terrain that was far from ideal for armor, the M113 displayed outstanding mobility, shock action and firepower. Its reliability was exemplary, while the protection it afforded, particularly in diesel-powered versions, was highly satisfactory considering its light armor. The success of many operations was directly attributable to the durability of this remarkable AFV.

M48A3

During the Vietnam war the standard medium tank used by US Army and Marine Corps armored units was the M48A3 Patton. Rugged and reliable, it gave sterling service from the time of its arrival in 1965 until the final battles of 1975. After the initial and deeply entrenched prejudice against the use of tanks in what was considered to be strictly an infantry or counter-insurgency war had been overcome, the M48A3 was given the opportunity to prove its value in support of infantry operations.

Despite problems of mobility in many areas of Vietnam, the firepower of the M48 was invaluable whenever the enemy was brought to battle. Few weapons were as effective against enemy bunkers. Although these field fortifications were proof against artillery rounds up to 155mm, close range tank fire was devastating. When tanks operated with infantry, their fire could be deployed much more quickly than artillery or air support, and their proximity facilitated communications and target indication. Such rapid response allowed the enemy no time to disengage. For this reason, the enemy often withdrew in the face of infantry supported by tanks— unless the tactical situation dictated otherwise, as in the defence of a base camp.

ABOVE
*The front of an M551
of 3/4th Cavalry lifts
off the ground as the
152mm main
armament is fired
during gunnery
training soon after the
arrival of the Sheridan
in Vietnam, February
1969. (US Army
CC54081)*

RIGHT
*An M551 Sheridan of
3rd Sqn., 4th Cavalry
moves out on one of its
first operations in
Vietnam, February
1969. The crew's fear
for the Sheridan's
vulnerability to RPGs
is indicated by the
screen mounted across
the hull front. Such
measures were soon
torn off when operating
in jungle. (US Army
CC55199)*

The majority of kills by tanks were made with canister or
'Beehive' and machine gun fire at close ranges. Only rarely were fields
of fire sufficient to use the main armament in a conventional long-
range capacity. This was demonstrated by the typical basic load of
90mm ammunition carried by the M48s of 1/69th Armor. After two
months of operations following arrival in Vietnam, the battalion
prescribed 24 HE, 20 canister, nine WP and nine HEAT. This
subsequently changed to 40 canister, 16 HE, four WP and two
HEAT. Some units carried as much as 80 per cent 'Beehive', 15 per
cent canister, and the remainder HE and WP.

As with most AFVs in Vietnam, field modifications were made to
increase the firepower of the M48A3. The most widespread of these
was the mounting of a .50 cal. M2HB Browning on the roof of the
commander's cupola. When fitted inside the M1 cupola the M2
machine gun lay on its left side, which made it difficult to operate. In
this location the gun's feed mechanism frequently jammed. Space
was at such a premium that only 100 rounds were available at one
loading, quite insufficient for a typical firefight. Since tank
commanders rarely closed their hatches, even in battle, most units
removed the .50 cal. from the cupola and mounted it on top. This was
generally accomplished by shortening the legs of an M3 tripod mount
and welding it in place. This arrangement overcame the operating
difficulties and allowed the use of longer belts of ammunition for
sustained firing. Other weapons included a .50 cal. in place of the
M73 7.62mm co-axial machine gun, and/or replacing the gunner's
M105C telescopic sight; a machine gun, either M2 or M60, close to
the loader's hatch; and a machine gun mounting at the back of the
turret for firing rearwards. The one aim of these modifications was to
achieve fire superiority as rapidly and over as wide an area as possible.

Some tanks were modified by mounting a 'cutting bar' across the
front of the vehicle, consisting of a dozer blade tip welded from
fender to fender. It proved an effective tool for clearing brush and
small trees, and was used to form access routes and helicopter landing

zones. Cutting jungle and brush with machetes and power saws was a time-consuming and back-breaking task. Crushing an area by the repeated passage of M48s was the fastest method, unless large trees were present. Even in the densest growth M48s could create an emergency LZ for a single Huey in under 15 minutes.

Movement through thick jungle for armor and infantry was painfully slow, progress being measured in hundreds of yards per hour. The M48A3 was highly effective in breaking trails through jungle growth for APCs and infantry, but continuous operation in heavy vegetation tended to overheat and damage the tank's transmission. As the jungle contained so many obstacles the traditional roles of armor and infantry were reversed, with the tanks leading. Infantry followed tanks at distances as great as 100 yards to minimise the risk from falling tree trunks and from booby-traps and mines. The enemy countered this tactic by hanging Claymore mines and explosives in the trees to explode at turret level, killing any exposed crew member. The devices were usually command-detonated, or else tripped by the tank's radio antenna. Tank crews countered this by travelling in wooded terrain with all antennae tied down and by firing 'prophylactic' rounds of canister into the trees.

As if these perils were not enough, Mother Nature added her own hazards for the unwary in the jungles of South-East Asia. The passage of AFVs through trees frequently dislodged ants' nests on to the vehicles. While the jungle was supposedly neutral, the ants apparently derived their ideological allegiance from their red colour. Even during the height of a firefight crewmen might be forced to abandon their vehicle, tearing off their clothing to escape the painful bites of 'chopper ants'. All tank crews carried aerosol cans of insecticide—forgetting them was comparable to forgetting to load up with ammunition! For the same reason, many AFVs carried a broom to brush ants off the exteriors of vehicles. Almost as dreaded as red ants were bees. A swarm of bees descending on a tank was no trivial matter, and several crews became seriously ill as a result of multiple stings. Among the ground-to-air signalling devices on AFVs, experienced crews always kept in reserve some green M18A1 smoke grenades: for some reason green smoke proved the best means of repelling bees, although no other colour seemed to work.

Besides insects, there was always the possibility of snakes dropping into an AFV. While a somnolent reticulated python falling into the back of an APC was a dramatic event, pythons were relatively harmless despite their length of up to 30 feet. The real danger came from the venomous snakes, there being numerous crannies in an AFV where they could hide to strike at any time. Most feared was the cobra, known by troops as the 'two-step', since that was commonly held to be as far as one could walk after being bitten. Tank crews took delight in crushing cobras (or any other snakes) beneath their tracks at every opportunity. The VC, capitalising on this fear, placed dead snakes coiled as if asleep on top of anti-tank mines. As a further instance of the jungle hazards, one tank commander was scarred for life around the face, chest and arms by an enraged monkey which fell on his turret roof.

Mines caused the greatest damage to the M48 in Vietnam. Tanks survived mine attack with few crew casualties, even when the enemy employed massive explosive devices made from unexploded aerial

The vulnerability of the M551 Sheridan to mine damage and RPG penetration led many units to reduce the crew to three men with no gunner inside the turret. The loader acted in his normal capacity during firefights, while the commander aimed and fired the main armament from his position. As contacts were invariably at close range, accuracy was not critical but speed of response was all-important, and crewmen outside the turret had a better view of fleeting targets and concealed enemy positions. An M551 Sheridan—plastered with graffiti—of Troop E, 1st Cavalry partakes in a search-and-destroy mission four miles south of the DMZ with 11th Inf. Bde., 23rd 'American' Div. in March 1971. (US Army SC662290)

OPPOSITE
Other units of the Free World Military Assistance Forces employed armor in Vietnam. The Royal Thai Army Expeditionary Division ('Black Panthers') incorporated 1st Armored Cavalry Sqn. equipped with M113 APCs. The Republic of Korea (ROK) Forces Vietnam Field Command comprised two divisions and a marine brigade. Denied permission to deploy a tank battalion, the Koreans acquired M113 APCs on permanent loan from the US, and these were employed as ACAVs in the Armor Regt. of the Capital Division.

bombs and artillery ordnance. Although damage to suspension components and vehicle fittings was extensive, the hull was rarely ruptured. Of course, given sufficient explosives any vehicle, however heavily armored, could be destroyed, and the industrious VC were forever seeking ways of luring tanks on to larger mines. The technique normally employed was for a concealed VC to snipe at a tank with an RPG from beyond its accurate range. This was done in the hope that the tank would come towards the sniper in a straight line—following the tactic of engaging the enemy wherever and whenever he was found. Along this line a mine was buried, often a 500lb. or 750lb. bomb, which was detonated as the tank passed over it by a second VC located at right angles. Such mines caused damage beyond local repair, and many tanks had to be returned to the United States to be refurbished.

In the minds of many crews the greatest threat to tanks was the RPG, whose penetrative power was frightening. On the other hand, anything that detonated the rocket before it struck the armor, be it a stowage box or spare track blocks, reduced the probability of penetration. M48s were consequently festooned with all manner of items. Track blocks, ration cartons, oil cans and used ammunition boxes were draped around the turret. Sponson boxes were filled with dirt; glacis plates were covered with sandbags; even PSP was hung over the sides to protect the suspension. Against the RPG-2 these measures were often effective, but little could be done to thwart the RPG-7. On penetration, the result varied between superficial and cataclysmic damage. A crewman in the direct path of the penetration might be killed or grievously wounded, while other crewmen were painfully, but not seriously, hurt by the spray of molten metal. Many were completely unharmed. Frequently, tanks fought on after one or more penetrations, unless the round caused a secondary explosion of fuel or ammunition. Nevertheless, the RPG was the scourge of

armor personnel in Vietnam. On a basis of cost and simplicity, it was
an extremely effective anti-armor weapon.

The dependable M48A3 was well liked by tank crews. There were
few automotive problems beyond those caused by the climatic
conditions of wet, dust and mud, and these were common to all AFVs
operating in Vietnam. Its ease of operation and ability to motor on
despite minimal maintenance was much appreciated.

The M60 Main Battle Tank was not employed in Vietnam,
although two of its derivatives did see service: the M728 Combat
Engineer Vehicle (CEV) and the M60 Armored Vehicle Launched
Bridge (AVLB). The latter replaced the M48A2 AVLB, which was
used initially in order to standardise on diesel-powered tanks for ease
of maintenance and reduced fire risk.

A Scorpion 90mm SPAT (Self-Propelled Anti-Tank Gun) and an APC of Co. D, 16th Armor of 173rd Airborne Brigade blast away at Viet Cong positions during an operation in Long Khanh Province, July 1966. This company was the only unit equipped with the SPAT during the war, and the only US Army Armor (as opposed to Cavalry) unit beside the three tank battalions—2/34th, 1/69th and 1/77th Armor—to serve in Vietnam. The SPAT was designed as an airborne assault vehicle, and shared the same chassis as the M76 Otter. It was superseded by the M551 Sheridan. (US Army SC633338)

In the summer of 1966 large scale combat operations in the Central Highlands put a severe strain on the motor transport units operating over the insecure road network in the Pleiku area. M113s were not always available for convoy escort, so truck units employed 'hardened vehicles' to provide the necessary security. 'HIGHLAND RAIDERS', a 'gun truck' based on a 2½-ton M35A2 of 64th Transportation Co., 8th Transportation Group (Motor Transport), operated out of Qui Nhon supplying units in the Central Highlands. (US Army Transportation Museum, Fort Eustis)

M551 SHERIDAN

Of all the AFVs employed in Vietnam, none was the subject of greater controversy than the M551 Sheridan. By designation it was an Armored Reconnaissance Airborne Assault Vehicle and not a tank, and the Sheridan's development and gestation was beset by mismanagement and compromise of the overly ambitious design criteria. Sheridan was conceived as a fire support weapon for airborne forces and as a cavalry reconnaissance vehicle. Its main armament was a 152mm gun-cum-missile launcher firing anti-tank guided missiles and a multi-purpose HEAT round with a combustible cartridge case. During development many difficulties arose with the guided missile and its complex electronics system, as well as the caseless ammunition. After several years of costly and largely futile attempts to resolve the many technical problems, the Army determined to test M551 in combat to ameliorate Congressional criticism of tank procurement procedures.

In January 1969 64 Sheridans arrived in Vietnam. As there were no suitable targets for an anti-tank round costing as much as a Rolls Royce motor car, they were deployed without guided missiles. Two armored cavalry squadrons—3rd Squadron, 4th Cavalry and 1st Squadron, 11th Armored Cavalry Regiment—were issued with the

OPPOSITE TOP
Armored units were obliged to provide convoy escort in Vietnam. Few missions were more disliked by armor personnel, as they involved long hours of monotonous motoring in extremes of weather and terrain under the constant threat of ambush and mine attack. Bearing the legend '52 TONS OF PURE DEATH' across the glacis plate, an M48A3 (Late Model) of 2/34th Armor escorts a convoy between Tay Ninh and Bear Cat. (Armor Magazine)

RIGHT
From the start, military convoys were escorted by armed jeeps and trucks. As casualties mounted, vehicles were sandbagged and armor-plated, but it was not until June 1967 that military police units received a suitable AFV for convoy escort and base security: the Cadillac Gage V-100 Commando Armored Car. Nicknamed 'the Duck' or simply the 'V', the Commando was a successful vehicle and was used by military police battalions and divisional MP units. A limited number of the earlier model XM-706 with a 7.62mm/.50 cal. machine gun combination in the turret was used by MP units, but most Commandos in US Army service were of the M706 type (formerly XM-706E1). Here, an M706 marked with the cartoon character Snoopy in an MP's helmet escorts a convoy bound for Qui Nhon during September 1970. Colourful cartoon characters were often painted on MP Commandos in Vietnam. (US Army SC658511)

M551, each receiving 27 vehicles. Few crewmen wanted the Sheridan, because it was suspected of being vulnerable to mines and RPGs, and lacking in the 'jungle busting' capability of the M48A3. This suspicion was proved to be correct all too soon.

In 3/4th Cav. Sheridan was substituted on a one-for-one basis for the M48A3s in cavalry platoons, whereas 11ACR issued three Sheridans in place of the two ACAVs in one of the cavalry platoon scout sections. Thus one unit exchanged a less capable vehicle for its M48A3s, while the other exchanged two ACAVs for three vehicles of greatly increased firepower. The Sheridans were ready for combat in the first week of February 1969.

Combat trials were conducted for a three-month period from 8 February to 8 May. The experiences of the two units varied, but both encountered difficulties with unreliable weapon components and mechanical deficiencies, many of which had been identified during trials conducted prior to deployment to Vietnam. These problems were compounded by a lack of spares, special tools and qualified instructors, notwithstanding the presence of manufacturer's representatives. Pressing combat commitments also reduced the time normally devoted to maintenance.

BELOW
The definitive model of the V-100 Commando was the M706 with twin 7.62mm M73 machine guns in the turret. It differed in detail from the version used by ARVN forces, with raised contour drivers' hatches, deletion of one vision block and one gun port along each side and 'Molotov cocktail' shield over the engine grille. These features are all evident in this photograph. Note the rearward-facing M60 for use by the radio operator. (John Graber)

An XM-706E2 armored car
patrols the perimeter of U-
Tapao airbase in Thailand
from where B52 bombers
undertook 'Arclight'
missions against targets in
Vietnam, September 1969.
Initially USAF police units
employed M151 utility
trucks for airbase defence
against sapper infiltration
and ground attack. To
satisfy the need for greater
firepower and armor
protection for Security
Alert Teams (SAT), the
USAF procured the M113
APC and the XM706E2.
This version of the V-100
Commando featured an
armored parapet with
folding doors, and carried a
variety of weapons including
M60 and M2 machine guns
or a 7.62mm minigun. The
XM706E2 served mainly as
a transport for a three-man
SAT, or as an ammunition
supply vehicle to perimeter
positions. It was highly
mobile and could traverse all
terrain in and around
airbases. By October 1969
approximately 60
XM706E2s and 30 M113s
were in service with USAF
security police units in
South-East Asia. (US Air
Force 106252)

On 15 February the first mine incident occurred. A Sheridan of 3/4th Cav. struck a 25lb. pressure-detonated mine. The explosion ruptured the hull and ignited the caseless ammunition, causing a catastrophic secondary explosion. The driver lost his life in the ensuing fire. Confidence in the Sheridan was severely shaken, as crews knew that a similar explosion under an M48A3 would only have blown off a road wheel or two. Had it occurred under an ACAV the vehicle would have been badly damaged, but secondary explosions would not have occurred and injuries would have been minor.

A measure of confidence was restored when, on the night of 10/11 March, Troop A, 3/4th Cavalry detected, by means of night observation devices, a group of enemy troops in an open field moving along a known infiltration route west of Ben Cui Rubber Plantation. The enemy were engaged with canister and the first round eliminated their command group. Having lost their leadership the enemy soldiers panicked and milled around the area only to be cut down by further rounds of canister. In a few minutes 42 of the enemy were killed, against two US soldiers wounded. This encounter demonstrated that Sheridan had considerable firepower even in the hours of darkness.

The main armament, however, suffered numerous problems. The principal deficiency was the caseless ammunition and its associated bore-scavenging system. A combustible cartridge case, self-consuming on firing, is an attractive concept, as it obviates the need for heavy brass shellcases and their subsequent disposal from the turret basket, where they exude noxious fumes. However, the caseless ammunition of Sheridan was highly inflammable and easily split or damaged, causing propellant to spill on to the turret floor—an

Three non-divisional artillery air defence battalions reactivated from Reserve and National Guard assets served in Vietnam, with one in each of Corps Tactical Zones I to III. They were 1st Bn. (Automatic Weapon Self-Propelled), 44th Artillery; 4/60th; and 5/2nd, in CTZ I to III respectively. Each battalion was augmented by a battery of truck-mounted M55 quad-.50 cal. machine guns. As a result their vehicles were dispersed over wide areas, but many units had cause to be grateful for the accurate automatic fire of Duster sections in support of a position under attack. An M42A1 Duster of 4/60th Artillery stands on the perimeter of an FSB in Dak To Province during Operation 'Greely', July 1967. (US Army CC41259)

By contemporary standards the M42A1 was obsolescent for its intended task of air defence; but in Vietnam, where there was no enemy air threat, it proved successful in the ground support role. Mounting twin 40mm Bofors guns on the modified chassis of the M41 light tank, the M42A1 was employed for convoy escort, point security and perimeter defence. Perched on a hill top overlooking Route 14 in the 'Marlboro Country' west of An Khe, a Duster of 4/60th Artillery 'puts out rounds' while a crewman adds his own contribution of firepower with an M16A1. (US Army SC650951)

LEFT
Mechanised artillery units employed a variety of self-propelled weapons in Vietnam. Certain field force artillery units were equipped with the M108 SP howitzer. Obsolescent, and replaced in Europe by the M109 as the direct support artillery for US armored and mechanised divisions, it remained on the field artillery inventory and was deployed to Vietnam. There it was used in the area support role or, if terrain permitted, in support of ground operations. Here an M108 of the Howitzer Battery, 3rd Sqn., 11 ACR is emplaced (with a tented bunker for ease of ammunition handling) in support of 1st Cav. Div. (Airmobile), October 1966. (US Army SC634558)

LEFT
The M107 Self-Propelled Gun was introduced into Vietnam in late 1965. The 175mm gun fired a 174lb. projectile to a range of 32 kilometres providing an umbrella of protection over wide areas. For the most part these heavy-calibre weapons remained in semi-permanent emplacements at fire support bases, as illustrated in this photograph of an M107 named 'ABORTION II' of Battery A, 8th Bn., 4th Artillery taken in March 1969. Only rarely did they travel by road, and then always with infantry and armor protection. (US Army SC649384)

ABOVE
The M107 proved a fine weapon but suffered from an extremely short tube life. After firing 300 full charge rounds (the average consumption of a gun every 45 days) it was necessary to replace the tube—a six-hour procedure until an enterprising 'redleg' in Vietnam devised a method to retain the nitrogen in the weapon's equilibrators during tube changes, which reduced the time to two hours as it was no longer necessary to replenish the lost gas. At one stage gun tubes were in such critically short supply that they had to be airlifted at great expense from the United States. Eventually, improved tube and ammunition design increased life expectancy to a manageable level. An ever-versatile M88 VTR changes the tube of an M107 of 2/32nd Artillery, September 1966. Artillery weapons were often named beginning with the battery letter, in this case 'CASSIUS' after the champion boxer, latterly Muhammed Ali. Expended 175mm gun tubes were partially buried across the roads of combat bases to restrict the speed of vehicle movement in such areas. (US Army SC633871)

123

BELOW
M109 Self-Propelled Howitzers and their supporting M548 Ammunition Resupply Vehicles of Bty. C, 2nd Bn., 138th Artillery take up firing positions during mobile operations near Phu Bai, July 1969. 2/138th Artillery was a National Guard unit from Kentucky, one of only two such field artillery battalions to serve in Vietnam. The M109 normally fought from prepared static positions but occasionally accompanied manoeuvre forces for direct support, as with 1st Bde., 5th Inf. Div. (Mechanized), or as an organic weapon with 11th Armored Cavalry Regiment. An M109 battery was sometimes committed to the direct support of a divisional cavalry squadron when it operated as an entity. The 155mm howitzer had a maximum range of almost 15 kilometres and fired a 95lb. projectile—or almost three times the weight of that of the 105mm. The M548 acted as an ammunition limber, incorporating a hoist and trolley to lift the heavy artillery 'projos'. (US Army SC651165)

OPPOSITE ABOVE
Lurking behind an RPG screen of cyclone fencing and mounting an ACAV turret, an M109 155mm Self-Propelled Howitzer of 8th Bn., 6th Artillery, of 1st Inf. Div. prepares to fire in support of ground troops of the 'Big Red One' at FSB Oklahoma, November 1969. With its high

unacceptable fire hazard. Vehicle vibration during cross-country movement cracked rounds stowed in the ammunition racks. The rounds were sensitive to moisture, oil and other contaminants, which caused them to swell to the extent that they would not seat properly in the breech. Damp rounds resulted in misfires or incomplete combustion, leaving smoldering residue in the breech. This could cause a subsequent round to detonate before the breech was closed, with catastrophic effect inside the turret. To overcome the problem the round was supplied sealed in a neoprene lining (a black rubber compound) to prevent moisture absorption, and in a further liner of white nine-ply nylon as ballistic protection when stored in the ammunition racks. In theory the loader simply peeled off the linings prior to loading a round into the breech; but in Vietnam crews usually stripped all the rounds before operations to speed up loading, so negating their effectiveness.

A Closed Breech Scavenging System (CBSS) was installed to overcome the problem of burning residue. This equipment comprised two air bottles (similar in appearance to fire extinguishers) inside the crew compartment, and a compressor. After each round was fired the system blew seven cubic feet of compressed air at a pressure of 650psi down the gun tube, clearing the breech of fumes

silhouette, the M109 was vulnerable to RPG attack. Standard cyclone fencing placed 20 to 25 feet in front of positions protected howitzers from rockets. Enemy sappers often attempted to penetrate fire support bases with the express intention of destroying these effective area weapons. During 1969, Division Artillery fired over one million rounds in support of the 'Big Red One'. (US Army SC653101)

An M110 named
'CASTRATOR' of 7th
Bn., 8th Artillery fires
in support of ground
operations, May 1968.
The 8in. howitzer fired
a 200lb. projectile
almost 17 kilometres,
and was the most
accurate weapon in the
field artillery. The
M110 was employed by
most division artilleries.
Whereas divisional
artillery supported
specific manoeuvre
operations, non-
divisional artillery
acted in an area support
role. Both the M110
and M107 served with
field force artillery; the
proportion varied
depending on the
tactical situation. Since
both weapons had
identical carriages, the
practice was to install
those tubes that best
met the current need.
One day a battery
might have all 175mm,
a few days later half
175mm and half
8-inch, or any
combination thereof.
(US Army
SC645662)

and any smoldering material. This action caused a characteristic plume of grey smoke and a distinctive hissing sound to be emitted after firing. The CBSS superseded an earlier open-breech system, since the latter blew burning residue into the turret as well as out of the barrel, with obviously unattractive consequences if there was any spilt propellant from ruptured rounds on the turret floor. Sheridans with CBSS had no bore evacuator fitted to the barrel, while those with the open-breech system did. Sheridans in Vietnam had the CBSS type.

Despite these problems, it must be stated that the majority of rounds fired left no residue, and their terminal effect on targets was devastating. The XM625 canister round won fearsome renown. Each 152mm 'Beehive' round contained on average 9,990 'flechettes', and some formidable kills were achieved; 3rd Squadron, 5th Cavalry recorded 36 enemy KiA from just two rounds. The XM409 multi-purpose HEAT was equally effective against bunkers and field fortifications. Firing a six-inch projectile from the 16-ton Sheridan caused massive recoil, lifting the front end some eighteen inches off the ground and the whole vehicle backwards two or three feet. Not only did crews have to brace themselves firmly to escape injury, but the forces imparted to the vehicle loosened bolts on many components.

It was unfortunate therefore that a number of other deficiencies soon became apparent during combat operations, the most prevalent being electrical power failures of the turret. Most were caused by

An M48A3 lies
burning as Viet Cong
troops man a 7.62mm
Goryunov SGMB
medium machine gun on
a Sokolov mount
during a battle at Dong
Rum, March 1967.
NVA and main force
VC units were well
equipped with highly
effective weapons at the
squad level, including
the RPG (Rocket
Propelled Grenade) for
anti-armor use and
against fortifications,
reliable medium
machine guns and the
excellent Kalashnikov
assault rifle. Until the
widespread use of the
M72 LAW, they
generally possessed
greater organic
firepower than their
opponents. (Socialist
Republic of Vietnam)

dust, damp or vibration which short-circuited electrical components. This problem was to plague Sheridan throughout its service in Vietnam, particularly during the wet season. Fan pullies and fanbelts broke repeatedly, leading to a total loss of electrical power until the inferior lightweight aluminium pullies were replaced by steel components and strengthened fanbelts substituted.

Most of the problems may be attributed to the Sheridan's precipitate combat debut, and many were overcome by the skill of maintenance personnel in the field. Teething troubles are experienced by all new AFVs: and by the conclusion of the test period the Sheridan proved to have greater mobility, firepower and night-fighting capability than the ACAV. After the initial problems with the fan pulleys and fanbelts automotive performance and reliability were good. In consequence, more Sheridans were sent to Vietnam. By late 1970 more than 200 were in theatre, and eventually almost every ground cavalry unit in Vietnam was equipped with them. However, their vulnerability to mine damage and RPG penetration remained a source of anguish to crews.

In late 1969 Troop A, 4th Squadron, 12th Cavalry of 1/5(Mech) Div. were issued with Sheridan. After wading the Qua Viet River on their first operation along the DMZ, three of the nine Sheridans struck mines which ruptured their hulls, detonating the caseless ammunition. Not unnaturally, the troopers of 4/12th Cav. were disinclined to venture on further operations until their remaining

Sheridans were fitted with 'belly armor'. Similar in concept to that fitted to ACAVs, the 'belly armor' of titanium plates strengthened the forward section of the vehicle floor and hull sponsons. All Sheridans in Vietnam were progressively fitted with this device, and replacement vehicles from factories came with it installed.

While 'belly armor' mitigated the effects of mine damage, RPG penetrations were disastrous. If the turret was pierced the main armament ammunition invariably detonated within 30 and often 15 seconds. Consequently, the crew of Sheridan abandoned their vehicle immediately after a hit, whereas the crew of an M48A3 often kept fighting. For this reason few gunners remained in the turret, preferring to 'ride shotgun' outside with an M79 grenade launcher or M60 machine gun. In these circumstances, the tank commander fired the main armament and co-axial machine gun from his position. Sheridan was highly vulnerable to RPGs to the very end. In March 1971 2nd Squadron, 11 ACR lost five in one action to RPG penetrations. All erupted into flames and were totally destroyed.

4 US MARINE CORPS ARMOR IN VIETNAM

The first operational use of tanks manned by Americans during the Vietnam War occurred in the first week of May 1965 when 2/3 Marines extended their TAOR from the immediate environs of Da Nang to encompass the village of Le My, a cluster of hamlets located on the southern bank of the Cu De River eight miles north-west of Da Nang airbase. During this first 'search and clear' operation with tanks, Marines encountered only sporadic sniper fire and suffered no casualties. Here, on 2 May, Marine 'ground-pounders' hitch a ride on an M48A3 of 2nd Platoon, Co. A, 3rd Tank Bn., which still retains the stub of its fording kit. (Tim Page)

The principal AFVs employed by the US Marine Corps in Vietnam were the M48A3s of Fleet Marine Force (FMF) Tank Battalions, the M50A1 Ontos of divisional Anti-Tank Battalions, and the LVTP-5 series of amphibious vehicles of FMF Amphibian Tractor Battalions.

Two Marine Tank Battalions, 1st and 3rd, served in Vietnam attached to 1st and 3rd Marine Divisions respectively. The primary role of the tank battalion was combat support during amphibious assault and subsequent operations ashore. In Vietnam, tanks were employed in direct support or under operational control of the infantry. The usual assignment was one tank company per infantry regiment. The regimental commander, in turn, assigned tank platoons to his battalions as required.

Marine tanks performed numerous tasks in Vietnam, the most important being direct support of infantry in the assault, perimeter defence, reaction force operations, strongpoint security, and convoy escort. They were also used in an artillery role, providing indirect and Harrassing and Interdiction fire.

During infantry operations the tanks undertook a variety of missions. Field fortifications and cave complexes were destroyed by direct fire. 'Reconnaissance by fire' thwarted ambushes and subdued enemy positions. Targets for aircraft and gunships were marked with white phosphorus (WP) shells—the most effective round for indicating targets to 'fast movers' (high performance aircraft in the close air support role). Tanks carried infantry and their stores during operations, with at least one squad assigned to accompany and protect each vehicle.

US Marine Corps
AFVs land in Vietnam
on 8 March 1965; the
first American armored
unit ashore was 3rd
Platoon, Company C,
3rd Anti-Tank
Battalion. An M50A1
Ontos rolls down the
ramp of an LCM-6 at
Red Beach 2, Da
Nang, in support of
Battalion Landing
Team (BLT) 3/9. On
the right front fender is
the three-pointed
caltrop insignia of 3rd
Marine Division.
(USMC A183793)

Direct fire support of infantry in attack was the primary role of Marine tanks. Firing main armament rounds into an enemy bunker system, an M48A3 of 'Charlie' Company, 1st Tank Bn. supports L/3/1 Marines in an assault south of Marble Mountain in March 1969. A Marine crouches on the engine decks indicating targets to the tank commander; a tank/infantry telephone with a 35ft. extension was fixed to the rear of the tank for just this purpose. (USMC A371899)

LEFT
M48A3 of 3rd Platoon, Co. A, 3rd Tank Bn., stands guard on LZ 'White' as a UH-34D 'Huss' of MAG-16 evacuates casualties during Operation 'Starlite', 18 August 1965—the first regimental-sized US combat action since the Korean War. At the outset of the operation the tanks made an amphibious landing, hence the deep-water fording kit fitted to this Patton. The 18in. searchlight is covered by a non-standard metal plate to protect the lens from small arms fire. (USMC A184966)

The variety of ammunition carried by tanks, their firepower, armor protection, superior communications and night-fighting capability added considerably to the defensive perimeter of any position. Likely avenues of enemy approach, critical terrain and other possible areas of enemy activity were plotted and registered during daylight and engaged with accuracy at night. A Xenon searchlight with infra-red capability was mounted co-axially above the 90mm gun, providing illumination of the defensive lines.

Tanks were continuously required to take part in reaction operations in order to relieve beleaguered forces. The NVA invariably anticipated such moves, and ambushes were prepared along obvious avenues of approach. In consequence Marine units planned alternative reaction routes whenever possible, with pre-planned air and artillery support. Tanks led reaction forces with their 90mm guns pointing left and right to cover the flanks. Cupola-mounted .50 cal. machine guns were traversed to cover the opposite direction. Depending on the situation and the rules of engagement for the particular area, 'reconnaissance by fire' was employed on the move. Upon reaching the objective the reaction force engaged the enemy if he had not already broken contact.

Outpost and strongpoint security involved the protection of important facilities such as bridges and priority roads. The static employment of tanks was wasteful, and such tasks were more profitably undertaken by other AFVs such as the Ontos. Tanks, however, could be used with decisive results, as in May 1968 when VC/NVA were repeatedly ambushing Route 561. 2/26 Marines and

*An M48A3 of 3rd
Tank Bn. fires in an
artillery role in support
of 2/4 Marines during
a search and destroy
mission in February
1968. Affixed to the
'gypsy rack' are four
40mm ammunition
boxes acquired from a
US Army Duster unit,
one for each crew
member. These
watertight containers
proved ideal for
carrying the crew's
personal possessions;
they comfortably
accommodated a sleeping
bag, airmatress, spare
dungarees and other
sundries, protecting
them from dust and
monsoon rains without
cluttering the interior of
the tank. Jerrycans
carried on the exterior
of vehicles contained
engine oil, water or
transmission fluid.
Marine tanks in
Vietnam were called
'Tigers' from their
radio callsign on 'clear
comms': this nickname
derived from the Esso
advertisement of the
time—'Put a tiger in
your tank'. A common
alternative was
'clanks'. (USMC
A650015)*

*An M48A3 of 1st
Platoon, Co. B, 3rd
Tank Bn. ploughs
through a maize field
during Operation
'Macon', July 1966, in
the 'Arizona
Territory'; this was an
agricultural area
desolated by war, lying
between the Vu Gia
and Thu Bon Rivers
north-west of An Hoa,
the scene of many fierce
firefights. Operation
'Macon' was no
exception: for three
months, five Marine
battalions consecutively*

*hounded the VC Doc
Lap Battalion, a main
force unit of great
tenacity and skill which
was particularly adept
at ambushes, mine
warfare, and sudden,
sharp ripostes against
unwary units up to
company size. Marine
tanks carried sufficient
C-rations on the
sponsons for three
days; those of the
attached infantry squad
were also carried, to
lighten their load.
(USMC A187263)*

*In Vietnam the tank
proved highly effective
in defence. Emplaced
on the perimeter at
Camp Carroll during
the Tet offensive of
February 1968, this
M48A3 is protected
from enemy mortar and
rocket fire by a barrier
of earth and sandbags.
Such well prepared
positions were only
customary at
permanent combat
bases. Near the tank is
the crew's 'hootch' or
living quarters, from
which a lanyard ran to*

*the manual trigger of
the main armament. At
night the gun was
loaded with a 'Beehive'
round set to explode
over the most likely
avenue of enemy
approach, so that in the
event of ground attack,
one round was 'on the
way' before the crew
even mounted the tank.
(USMC A190762)*

135

One of the standard missions for Marine tanks was to provide security for motor transport convoys, known in Marine jargon as 'Rough Rider' operations. Supported by 'grunts' of 3/4 Marines, a Patton of 3rd Tank Bn. leads a convoy behind a patrol sweeping for mines along Route 9 west of Con Thien in July 1967. Unit SOP dictated that the tow cables were permanently attached at the front and rear and stowed across the glacis plate in the manner shown. This allowed infantry to connect a disabled or knocked out tank without the crew having to dismount, the crew in turn providing covering fire to the infantry. (USMC A189063)

the tanks of Tank Force Mike were committed to protect the road. A series of observation posts and infantry positions was established with two mutually-supporting strongpoints, each of one tank and an infantry squad, on high terrain to the west of the road. Moving out at dawn each day with engineer minesweeping teams, the tanks occupied their vantage points prior to traffic being released along the road. Artillery fire was registered on avenues of enemy movement and for protection of the outposts. At dusk, traffic ceased, and the two tank/infantry teams returned to their defensive positions at Cam Lo. 'H-and-I' fire was called from time to time during the night to discourage VC mining efforts. Enemy ambushes along Route 561 ceased as long as the strongpoints were maintained.

Tanks provided security for convoys plying between logistical areas and combat bases. Being predominantly roadbound, the tanks were highly susceptible to enemy mining. They always operated in pairs (the minimum on any operation in Vietnam) since two tanks were mutually supporting, and if one was hit or broke down the other could tow it to a safe area. Tactics for convoy protection were similar to those for reaction forces. During Operation 'Cumberland' in June 1967, 1/4 Marines were clearing Route 547 in order to establish a fire base some 17 miles west of Phu Bai to counter the enemy presence in the A Shau Valley. The road was in poor condition, winding, steeply banked and continually mined by the enemy. Thick vegetation grew right up to the road edges. Enemy mines and ambushes had taken a grim toll of Marines and vehicles. To ensure the passage of vitally needed supplies, 1/4 Marines adopted 'shoot and move' tactics along

the road. Supporting artillery was organised to cover the flanks of the column and to precede the advance by a suitable safety margin. A tank section led the convoy, armed with predominantly canister ammunition. Moving by leaps and bounds, covering each other at all times, the tanks fired on every likely ambush site. A flame tank accompanied the column and burned away heavy brush from the edges of the road. Infantry rode on the tanks, sitting aft of the gun sights so as not to impede tank reaction time. Enemy activity along Route 547 was much reduced by these tactics.

The M48A3 was employed to supplement defensive fire plans, but because of the flat trajectory of the 90mm gun it was not well suited for indirect fire. Nevertheless, tanks were widely used in this role during the wet season when mobile operations were curtailed by mud. Tanks fired on targets as directed by the infantry. The main problems with indirect tank fire were the lack of organic fire direction control and observed effect. Despite these shortcomings, however, Marine tanks frequently executed night 'H-and-I' fires. A typical mission involved a section of tanks or Dusters firing a predetermined number of rounds at irregular intervals into a designated grid square to deter enemy activity during the hours of darkness. These fire plans consumed large amounts of ammunition, resulting in rapid trunnion and barrel wear. The tube life of the 90mm gun was generally about 1,600 rounds, depending on the quantity of canister fired.

Marine tanks have traditionally supported infantry operations employing tactics evolved during the Second World War (primarily at Okinawa) and re-emphasised during the Korean War. Tactics

Variously known as 'Zippos' or 'flames', the M67A2s were a fearsome weapon against Buddhists, to whom death by fire is anathema—and there were many Buddhists even in the forces of atheistic Communism. The psychological effect of these weapons was not exploited fully; more often than not, 'flames' were confined to base camps, where they were used to burn away vegetation clogging the perimeter wire, or even for such housekeeping duties as burning garbage! (USMC A187551)

RIGHT BELOW
In a typical task for Marine armor, an M67A2 flamethrower of Headquarters and Service Company, 3rd Tank Bn. stands guard on the perimeter of a 'ville', 1965. The shorter and thicker tube of the M7A1-6 flame gun, compared to the standard 90mm gun, is apparent in this photograph. Maximum range for a 60-second 'rod' (flame) was 250 yards, but 100 to 150 yards was the most effective distance, using ten- to 20-second 'rod' bursts. Available firing time varied between 55

and 61 seconds depending on the adjustment size of the nozzle bore; when the flame fuel had been expended the vehicle's armament was restricted to its machine guns. For this reason its value on extended operations was limited, as no unit wished to provide the essential escort to accompany the flame tank back to base in order to refuel. Note the compressor tubing to fuel and pressurise the flame tanks lashed to the turret rack. (USMC A186353)

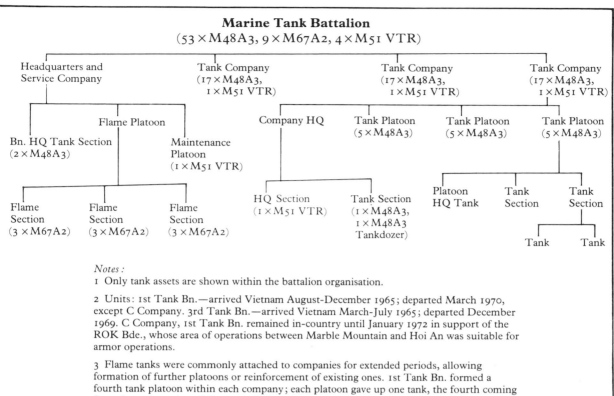

Marine Tank Battalion
(53 × M48A3, 9 × M67A2, 4 × M51 VTR)

- Headquarters and Service Company
  - Bn. HQ Tank Section (2 × M48A3)
  - Flame Platoon
    - Flame Section (3 × M67A2)
    - Flame Section (3 × M67A2)
    - Flame Section (3 × M67A2)
  - Maintenance Platoon (1 × M51 VTR)
- Tank Company (17 × M48A3, 1 × M51 VTR)
  - Company HQ
    - HQ Section (1 × M51 VTR)
    - Tank Section (1 × M48A3, 1 × M48A3 Tankdozer)
  - Tank Platoon (5 × M48A3)
  - Tank Platoon (5 × M48A3)
  - Tank Platoon (5 × M48A3)
    - Platoon HQ Tank
    - Tank Section
    - Tank Section
      - Tank
      - Tank
- Tank Company (17 × M48A3, 1 × M51 VTR)
- Tank Company (17 × M48A3, 1 × M51 VTR)

Notes:

1 Only tank assets are shown within the battalion organisation.

2 Units: 1st Tank Bn.—arrived Vietnam August-December 1965; departed March 1970, except C Company. 3rd Tank Bn.—arrived Vietnam March-July 1965; departed December 1969. C Company, 1st Tank Bn. remained in-country until January 1972 in support of the ROK Bde., whose area of operations between Marble Mountain and Hoi An was suitable for armor operations.

3 Flame tanks were commonly attached to companies for extended periods, allowing formation of further platoons or reinforcement of existing ones. 1st Tank Bn. formed a fourth tank platoon within each company; each platoon gave up one tank, the fourth coming from the tank section of Company HQ.

An M50A1 Ontos crushes a hedgerow as it moves forward in support of an infantry unit during Operation 'Mobile' in the Chu Lai area, May 1966. It was common practice for crews to mark their personal equipment, such as CVC helmets and flak-jackets, with the vehicle number. This not only enhanced unit éspirit, but also discouraged pilfering by other vehicle crews! The markings indicate the first vehicle of 1st Platoon, Co. C, 1st Anti-Tank Battalion. The driver has piled sandbags around his hatch to augment the thin armor. The commander has similarly placed sandbags beneath the M1919A4 Browning, to protect his midriff when firing the machine gun from his exposed position. Most Ontos carried spare track across the glacis plate as further protection, and because it was always in short supply. Beneath the spare track is the ubiquitous box of combat rations carried on all operations in 'the boonies'. (USMC A369169)

changed little in Vietnam prior to the Tet offensive of 1968, and became increasingly predictable. The standard assignment of tanks to infantry was a platoon of five tanks to the battalion. Once attached, they were further divided into two or three tank sections. Tanks and infantry normally attacked on a single integrated axis. This doctrinal fragmentation of tank units dictated that the offensive firepower and shock action of tanks in the assault was rarely exploited to the full. Except for certain areas of I Corps, such as 'Leatherneck Square' or the 'Arizona Territory', the terrain did not favour tank movement; and in those areas where mobile operations were possible the enemy was careful never to expose himself to tanks except in places and at times of his own choosing.

As elsewhere in Vietnam mining and RPG ambushes were the principal VC/NVA anti-tank tactics. In Thua Thien Province, the VC resorted to skilful 'nuisance mining'. In addition to box mines, which were difficult to detect, the VC used unexploded artillery rounds and aircraft bombs, usually command-detonated. The NVA in northern I Corps also used mines but to a lesser extent and normally covered by fire. RPGs were employed to reinforce an ambush. Terrain selection was invariably masterly. Movement was difficult and deployment for tanks often impossible. Fords, narrow passes and bends in the road were frequently utilised. A command-detonated mine triggered the ambush, followed by a hail of RPGs. Anti-tank mines were rarely encountered on cross-country operations, but anti-personnel mines and booby traps were often hastily rigged in the path of Marine infantry. Anti-tank mines were mostly emplaced along Main Supply Routes and in the vicinity of base camps.

Both VC and NVA mine warfare techniques won the grudging respect of the Marines. After several weeks 'in-country' tank crews developed a nose for mines and ambushes. Any disruption of civilian traffic flow along a particular road was a good indicator of VC mining. 'Reconnaissance by fire' was employed north of the '62-grid line', and often disrupted enemy plans. Below the '62-grid line', 'rules of engagement' applied in order to protect civilian lives and property, and 'recon by fire' was curtailed. Engineer minesweeping teams were successful in discovering some mines, but the toll in tanks and other vehicles remained high. Crews rapidly became proficient in field repairs of suspensions.

When the full fury of the enemy Tet offensive broke in I Corps area on 30 January 1968, the Marine divisions were widely dispersed. The fire base concept was in use at battalion level. It soon became apparent that 6th NVA Regiment (a division-size unit of at least eight battalions) had infiltrated the vicinity of Hue City, while NVA 324B Division was in strength from Khe Sanh to Cua Viet, and 2nd NVA Division was preparing for a full scale offensive against Da Nang. Maj. Gen. R. Tompkins, commanding general 3rd Marine Division, appreciated the need for a divisional reserve capable of striking at enemy concentrations in all directions, as well as supporting the major fire bases should they be attacked. A mobile task force was formed under the command of Col. Clifford B. Robichaud, from whom the unit took its title—'Task Force Robbie'. This comprised a reinforced infantry battalion, two tank companies of 3rd Tank Battalion, an Ontos platoon, two sections of US Army M55 'quad

An M53 Self-Propelled Gun of 1st 155 Gun Battery (SP) fires on enemy positions February 1967. These massive vehicles were part of Fleet Marine Force artillery, and were deployed to assist divisional artillery when increased ranges or delivery capabilities were needed. FMF artillery also included the 8in. self-propelled howitzer: both systems served in Vietnam. The M55s of 1st 8-in. Howitzer Battery (SP) were replaced by the M110s during 1967. (USMC A188930)

An M51 Heavy
Recovery Vehicle of
3rd Tank Bn.
disembarks from an
LCM-8 'Mike 8 Boat'
at the Dong Ha ferry
across the Cua Viet
River, June 1967. Four
of these superb vehicles
supported each Marine
tank battalion, one per
company. Commonly
referred to as 'retriever'
or 'ox' from its radio
callsign, the M51's
only disadvantage was
the gargantuan fuel
consumption of its

gasoline-powered
engine. The VC/NVA
were well aware of the
importance of the M51,
and enemy sappers
made every effort to
penetrate perimeters
and destroy these
vehicles. 3rd Tank Bn.
lost two to enemy action
during the war.
(USMC A188836)

RIGHT
The ungainly
appearance of the
Ontos is all too
apparent in this 1966

photograph of an
M50A1 of Co. A, 1st
Anti-Tank Bn with its
106mm recoilless rifles
at maximum elevation
in the fire support role.
A major limitation was
the necessity to reload
the rifles from outside
the vehicle, exposing
the crew to enemy fire.
The M8 .50 cal.
spotting rifles can be
seen above the four top
recoilless rifles, while
rifles 2 and 5 (upper
outboard) each had a
direct fire sight as well

as a spotting rifle
attached. These two
rifles could be removed
and installed on a
ground mount if
necessary. All weapons
were aligned and
controlled from inside
the vehicle, using a
periscope sight, and
fired electrically. On
the right front fender is
a porcine cartoon and
the name 'BACON',
illustrative of the
vehicle's Vietnam
nickname of 'Pig'.
(USMC A373659)

ABOVE LEFT
As enemy infiltration across the DMZ increased during 1966, Marine artillery assets were too few to cover the whole region, so US Army field artillery battalions were introduced into I Corps to provide additional support, including 2/94th Artillery equipped with M107 175mm self-propelled guns. With their increased range these heavy weapons could provide artillery coverage from the Gulf of Tonkin to Laos, reducing enemy freedom of movement along the DMZ. From March 1969 the M53 was superceded by the M107 in FMF artillery; the photograph shows one of the first fire missions conducted by USMC 175mm SP guns in Vietnam. (USMC A371926)

BELOW LEFT
Encircled by laterite-filled shell casings and ready-rounds, an M109 155mm Self-Propelled Howitzer of Bty. M, 4/12 Marines fires on enemy positions near Phu Bai in October 1966. Prior to the Vietnam War the M109 replaced the M114A1 155mm towed howitzer to enhance the mobility of Marine divisional artillery regiments. As the need for more artillery grew, the old towed weapons were shipped to Vietnam. Ironically, the obsolescent M114A1 proved to have greater mobility, as it could be moved by helicopter and truck while the heavy M109, being too valuable to expose to the risk of RPGs and mines, was confined to an essentially static role in fire support bases. (USMC A188024)

ABOVE
Transporting riflemen of 2/3 Marines, amtracs negotiate a river during a 'sweep' ten miles north of Da Nang airbase, June 1965. Many operations were conducted at this distance from airbases as this was the optimum range of Communist free-flight rockets, and Marines constantly searched for the launch sites that formed the 'Rocket belt'. The box-like 'doghouse' on the rear decks is the exhaust and air intake housing, the principal external identifying feature of the LVTP-5A1 model. The markings identify the ninth vehicle of 3rd Platoon, Co. B, 1st Amphibian Tractor Battalion. The yellow shield between the 'B' and number '39' is a tactical insignia of FMF troops and is inscribed '1 LVT' in red. Note the Helmet MC-2 of the amtrac driver in the foreground. (USMC A184621)

50s', a battery of M42A1 Dusters of 1/44th Artillery, and supporting elements including a communications platoon with American Indian speakers to ensure 'secure comms'. All units were truck- or jeep-mounted with added protection of sandbags and armor plating.

The task force base camp was located at Cam Lo on the south-west corner of 'Leatherneck Square'. When the tanks and vehicles rolled into the area they 'circled the wagons', assuming a defensive posture and began planning for assault or reaction operations. Reconnaissance elements were introduced by helicopter and ground patrols, collecting vital intelligence to enable mobile operations to be implemented. A series of 'strike routes' was formulated, and it was discovered that with some engineer effort it was possible to mass Task Force Robbie at any point in the area of operations. Since no artillery was attached, artillery support was arranged with pre-planned fire missions along the strike routes from neighbouring fire bases.

As the Tet offensive waned the need for a mobile divisional reserve lessened. The war in I Corps reverted to the infantry and an 'enclave strategy'. Task Force Robbie was disbanded in June 1968; but this was the first occasion that the concept of mobile warfare with an armor-orientated formation was used in combat by the Marines, and for that reason Task Force Robbie will remain significant.

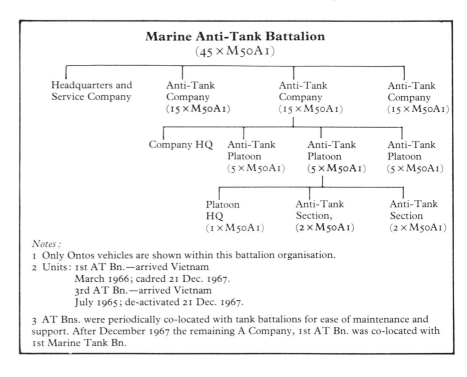

Marine Anti-Tank Battalion
(45 × M50A1)

Headquarters and Service Company — Anti-Tank Company (15 × M50A1) — Anti-Tank Company (15 × M50A1) — Anti-Tank Company (15 × M50A1)

Company HQ — Anti-Tank Platoon (5 × M50A1) — Anti-Tank Platoon (5 × M50A1) — Anti-Tank Platoon (5 × M50A1)

Platoon HQ (1 × M50A1) — Anti-Tank Section, (2 × M50A1) — Anti-Tank Section (2 × M50A1)

Notes:
1 Only Ontos vehicles are shown within this battalion organisation.
2 Units: 1st AT Bn.—arrived Vietnam
         March 1966; cadred 21 Dec. 1967.
         3rd AT Bn.—arrived Vietnam
         July 1965; de-activated 21 Dec. 1967.

3 AT Bns. were periodically co-located with tank battalions for ease of maintenance and support. After December 1967 the remaining A Company, 1st AT Bn. was co-located with 1st Marine Tank Bn.

M50A1 ONTOS
The ungainly-looking Ontos ('The Thing' in Greek) was a lightly armored tracked vehicle mounting six M40A1C 106mm recoilless rifles, four M8 .50 cal. spotting rifles and an M1919A4 .30 cal. machine gun. Its primary mission was the destruction of enemy armor, but in the absence of such a threat it provided direct support for the infantry. In Vietnam, it was employed for perimeter defence, convoy escort and fire support on infantry operations.

*Leathernecks of 2/4
Marines cross the Qua
Viet River by
amphibian tractors
during Operation
'Saline II' near Dong
Ha, March 1968. By
this time many amtracs
carried sandbag
emplacements for a
machine gun forward of
the M1 turret. The
turret design allowed
only limited depression
of the machine gun and
its position resulted in a
wide area of 'dead
ground' to the front of
the vehicle. The
LVTP-5A1 was
designed to transport a
maximum of 34 combat-
loaded troops, with 25
as the optimum.
(USMC A194604)*

'From the halls of Montezuma to the sands of . . . Red Beach 2, Da Nang, South Vietnam. LVTP-5A1s of 3rd Platoon, Co. A, 1st Amphibian Tractor Bn. land Marines of BLT 3/4 on 14 April 1965. Besides its role as a troop transport the LVTP-5A1 was employed as a cargo carrier, with six tons of stores when afloat and nine tons on land; as an artillery prime mover or carrier capable of carrying a 105mm howitzer complete with crew, 90 rounds of ammunition and ancillary equipment; and as an amphibious ambulance—with the medical kit installed the LVT provided capacity for 12 stretcher cases, medical equipment and corpsmen. The latter role occurred most often during the monsoon season, when 'P-5s' were restricted to roads and combat bases where they were converted to static medical aid posts. (USMC A183933)*

Its service was undistinguished, except on a few notable occasions. This was for a number of reasons, the primary factor being a lack of understanding of its full capabilities. Each major supporting arm in the Marine Corps is represented by a particular Military Occupational Speciality (MOS): thus, Marines who serve in tanks have 'MOS 1802', and those in amphibian tractors '1806'. Each Marine retains his MOS throughout his career and so becomes totally familiar with its particular weapons and their methods of employment. No such MOS applied in Marine anti-tank battalions, so all the officers were infantrymen except for the executive officer who was a 'tanker'. Frequently assigned to an anti-tank battalion for a single tour, few infantry officers developed a thorough understanding of Ontos or of armor tactics. Consequently there was little corporate knowledge or enthusiasm for the vehicle.

Ontos was initially used in road convoys, but because of its hazardous backblast on firing its value to the column was limited. This shortcoming was compounded by several accidental discharges while on convoy escort, with disastrous effect to the vehicle directly ahead. These accidents were caused by the firing cable, sear and trigger working improperly, either separately or together. If the firing cable was adjusted too tightly, vehicle vibration could cause the firing mechanism to release. These accidental firings caused restrictions to be placed on the vehicle, limiting its value as a support weapon.

On mobile operations the Ontos had adequate cross-country mobility, and because of its light weight was able to negotiate the flimsy bridges encountered in Vietnam. However, lack of trained crews led to inadequate maintenance; and the shortage of spare parts, especially track, resulted in recurrent breakdowns on operations. Its low ground pressure allowed it to negotiate many flooded paddy fields impassable to other tracked vehicles. During one operation in 1966 tanks became mired in mud following heavy rains. Unaffected by the terrain, Ontos were used to drag up timbers necessary to recover the stranded tanks.

Ontos had only light armor protection and was unsuited for the direct assault of defended positions. The vehicle was fearfully vulnerable to mines, which led to a further decline in its use. During an operation west of Hue an Ontos ran over a 500lb. bomb. The vehicle and crew disintegrated, parts being found half a mile away. As a result Ontos were relegated to static emplacements on perimeter defences. On some occasions, however, it did achieve success, notably during the battle of Hue City, when a determined unit gave invaluable fire support even in an urban area.

LVTP-5A1 AMPHIBIAN TRACTOR

In the US Marine Corps all amphibian vehicle units are organic elements of Force Troops, Fleet Marine Forces, and are normally organised as Amphibian Tractor Battalions. These units support a landing force both tactically and logistically. In Vietnam amphibian tractor battalions were attached to 1st and 3rd Marine Divisions of III MAF. Through an anomaly of deployment after the Korean War, 1st Amphibian Tractor Battalion was assigned to 3rd Marine Division and 3rd Amphibian Tractor Battalion to 1st Marine Division.

Their principal equipment was the LVTP-5A1 (Landing Vehicle, Tracked, Personnel) and its derivatives. Commonly known as 'amtracs' from 'amphibian tractors', they were used extensively in Vietnam for a variety of tasks in support of infantry battalions. Besides their primary function of transporting Marines to assault beaches (although there were no opposed landings in Vietnam), they were used early in the war as substitutes for armored personnel carriers during infantry operations on land. (The Marine Corps did not possess the M113 APC.) This proved too dangerous, for between the hull floor and deck plates were located 12 fuel cells containing a

There were four major derivatives of the LVTP-5: the 'C-1', 'E-1', 'H-6' and 'R-1'. All served in the Vietnam War. The 'R-1'—or to give it its full designation, Landing Vehicle Tracked, Recovery, Model 1 (LVTR-1A1)—was employed for the repair and retrieval of other amtracs. A 'retriever' of the Maintenance Platoon, Co. B Headquarters of 3rd Amphibian Tractor Bn. 'pulls an engine' of a 'P-5' for repairs at the battalion's base near Marble Mountain in 1968. Note the 'doghouse' and top-plate resting on the oil drums in the foreground; and forward of the 'Call Girl' cartoon the six-pointed star common to all amtracs, which was an indicator of the safe waterline level when afloat, but was ignored on operations. (USMC A194570)

151

total of 456 gallons of 80-octane gasoline. When a mine was struck the resulting secondary explosion and fire immolated anyone travelling inside. For this reason, Marine riflemen always sat on the outside of the vehicle with cargo lining the floor.

Thereafter, amtracs were rarely employed on offensive operations other than along the coastline or on negotiable rivers. As part of the 'Brown Water Navy' they interdicted enemy rivercraft and conducted sweeps for rocket sites around airbases. Their most common task in the later stages of the war was as supply vehicles between battalion areas and outlying positions. Troops were transported to the 'line of departure' of an operation, and limited fire support was provided with the .30 cal. machine gun. The M1 machine gun cupola on amtracs was ineffective in Vietnam. It had been designed for

A 'blooper man' reloads his M79 grenade launcher as Marines advance under covering fire from an LVTH-6A1 of 1st Provisional Armored Amphibian Tractor Platoon against entrenched enemy automatic weapons during Operation 'Arizona', June 1967. This unit comprised one LVTP-5A1(CMD), one LVTP-5A1, and six LVTH-6A1s divided into 'heavy sections' of three or 'light sections' of two depending on the mission and tactical situation. A typical task was as an escort to amtracs on a resupply run, when the firepower of the 105mm howitzer proved an effective counter to ambushes. The 1st PAAP was formed at Da Nang in 1965 for six months of combat trials. During its service in Vietnam the platoon fired more than 200,000 rounds, and remained 'in-country' until 1972 in support of the ROK 2nd Marine Bde.—the 'Blue Dragons'. (USMC A371185)

This remarkable
sequence of photographs
depicts an LVTE-1 of 3rd
Amphibian Tractor
Bn. firing its 'Zuni'
rocket-propelled
demolition line charge,
followed by detonation.
This equipment was
used to clear a path
through minefields
across an assault beach
for following amtracs;
the E-1 fired an M125
line charge to its front,
the demolitions then
exploding on the ground
and setting off the
mines. On this
particular mission
multiple line charges
were laid across the
target area and
detonated
simultaneously.
(Private collection)

RIGHT
*The M76 Otter
Amphibious Cargo
Carrier was designed as
the replacement for the
redoubtable M29C
Weasel which had
served the French so
well during the First
Indo-China War. This
marginal terrain
vehicle was intended to
transport general cargo
and personnel on land
or water, and proved
especially useful in
extensive base areas
where it carried
supplies to far-flung
perimeter positions, but
its lack of armor
protection limited its
value on mobile
operations. Here an
M76 of the Otter
Platoon, H and S Co.,
3rd Motor Transport
Bn. patrols the
perimeter at Khe Sanh
Combat Base, January
1968, where they
suffered the faintly
ludicrous situation of
tracked vehicles being
rendered inoperative by
flat tyres when the
pneumatic wheels were
repeatedly punctured
by artillery fragments.
Note the ace of spades
playing card in the
helmet band of the
Marine at the .50 cal.
Browning, and the
spade symbol on the
vehicle's nose and door.
This device was
erroneously believed by
many Marines, and
indeed many other
American units in
Vietnam, to strike
mortal fear into the
hearts of the Viet
Cong. It was often
adorned with such
slogans as 'Sat Cong'—
'death to Communism'.
(USMC A190444)*

suppressive fire from water level during amphibious assaults, where it performed well. On land, however, it was difficult to spot a target through the vision blocks while in motion, and even harder to train the gun on a fleeting enemy by frantically turning the handcrank of the heavy cupola, which frequently jammed during violent cross-country movement. Moreover, no crewman wished to be confined in the cupola for fear of mine explosion. Consequently a sandbag emplacement was arranged on top of amtracs, with an M1919 or M60 laid across it.

Amtracs also formed part of Special Landing Forces (SLF). Several types of amphibious operations were conducted during the Vietnam War employing either 'in-country' units of III MAF, forces of US Seventh Fleet or a combination of both. All were different in concept and execution depending on the tactical situation, but normally an SLF was structured around an infantry battalion, a helicopter squadron, a tank platoon and an Ontos platoon. In addition, amtracs engaged in the ship-to-shore role, inserting or extracting troops and landing supplies in support of operations.

The purpose of SLF operations was to strike swiftly from the sea at enemy concentrations on the coast. The enemy was careful not to offer a profitable target below the DMZ to amphibious forces, and the operations were often little more than 'a walk in the sun'. Two SLFs were created, Alpha and Bravo, and they achieved some success during Operation 'Market Time', the continuous Navy and

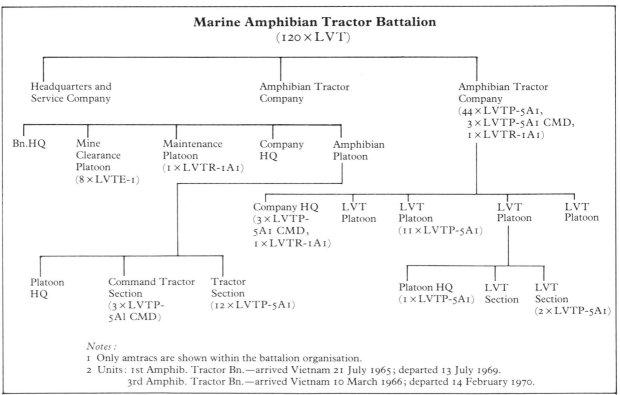

Marine Amphibian Tractor Battalion
(120 × LVT)

Headquarters and Service Company

Amphibian Tractor Company

Amphibian Tractor Company
(44 × LVTP-5A1,
3 × LVTP-5A1 CMD,
1 × LVTR-1A1)

Bn.HQ

Mine Clearance Platoon
(8 × LVTE-1)

Maintenance Platoon
(1 × LVTR-1A1)

Company HQ

Amphibian Platoon

Company HQ
(3 × LVTP-5A1 CMD,
1 × LVTR-1A1)

LVT Platoon

LVT Platoon
(11 × LVTP-5A1)

LVT Platoon

LVT Platoon

Platoon HQ

Command Tractor Section
(3 × LVTP-5A1 CMD)

Tractor Section
(12 × LVTP-5A1)

Platoon HQ
(1 × LVTP-5A1)

LVT Section

LVT Section
(2 × LVTP-5A1)

Notes:
1 Only amtracs are shown within the battalion organisation.
2 Units: 1st Amphib. Tractor Bn.—arrived Vietnam 21 July 1965; departed 13 July 1969.
   3rd Amphib. Tractor Bn.—arrived Vietnam 10 March 1966; departed 14 February 1970.

BATTLE OF HUE—TET 1968

OPPOSITE ABOVE
An M48A3, ironically named 'THE ORIGINAL FLOWER CHILDREN', supports 1/5 Marines, 12 February 1968. A company of 1/5 Marines supported by 3rd Platoon, Co. A, 1st Tank Bn. and several Ontos vehicles arrived at the 1st ARVN Division compound on the night of 11 February. On the 12th 1/5 Marines attacked towards the walled city, two-thirds of which was still occupied by the enemy. The fighting of the next ten days was both sustained and intense. The

tanks were in constant demand, often expending their complete ammunition loads within hours. Although struck repeatedly by RPG-2s, they continued to fight despite extensive damage, especially to optical equipment and radio antennae. Tank crews were so shaken by multiple hits that crew members were changed as often as once a day. (USMC A194565)

ABOVE
Refugees stream past an M67A2 during the battle for Hue, 3 February 1968. The first Marine tanks to enter the city were two M48A3s and two M67A2 flamethrower tanks of H & S Co., 3rd Marine Tank Bn. These tanks were sucked into the battle while driving from Phu Bai to the Hue landing craft ramp for transportation to Dong Ha. Accompanied by two Dusters of 1/44th

Artillery, they supported Co. G, 2/5 Marines and the command group of 1/1 Marines as they battled forward south of the Perfume River to relieve the MACV compound which was under attack by 804th Bn. of 4th NVA Regt. For 11 days these four tanks were the only Marine armor in the city until relieved by a platoon from 1st Tank Battalion. One tank was destroyed. (USMC A371336)

LEFT ABOVE
Under the leaden skies
which prevented air support
for much of the battle, an
M48A3 grinds forward
closely accompanied by an
M60 team of 1/5 Marines
beside the bullet-pocked
walls of the Imperial City,
12 February 1968. Typical
of the fighting in Hue, the
narrow street restricts the
advance to a single tank
frontage, denying the
benefits of mutual support.
However, this allowed tanks
to pivot in the middle of a
street to provide cover to
infantry crossing from one
side to the other. Tanks
often proved to be the only
means of evacuating
casualties from the bullet-
swept streets. Along the gun
barrel is the tank name 'MAD
HARLOT' in flawless Gothic
script. The vehicle number
'A51' identifies the tank of
'Alpha' Company
commander, while the
tactical insignia on the
glacis plate indicates 1st
Tank Battalion. Forward of
the coincidence rangefinder
housing 'rabbit ear' is a
'body count' tally of two

leering oriental faces in
yellow under conical hats
adorned with red stars.
(USMC A190583)

LEFT BELOW
The Ontos proved highly
effective in the battle of Hue
in a role for which it was
never intended. The
accurate fire of its 106mm
recoilless rifles was
devastating against enemy
emplacements, when
political considerations
dictated that only direct-fire
weapons be used to minimise
damage to the historic
buildings of Hue. The enemy
fortified many houses with
sandbags behind windows
and doors. To prevent such
bunkers delaying the
advance of the infantry, an
Ontos would move forward
and fire a HEAT round just
below the windowsill,
followed by a HEP round
through the hole to explode
in the heart of the position.
'Beehive' rounds were
extensively employed, both
for anti-personnel use and,
due to a lack of WP, as a
smokescreen for infantry
sprinting across the streets.

Firing a 'Beehive' round
into the plaster walls of
houses produced a cloud of
dust which effectively
screened infantry movement.
Here, an Ontos of 3rd
Platoon is replenished with
ammunition in a courtyard
adjacent to the MACV
Compound, 11 February
1968. The Ontos unit in the
battle of Hue was A Co.
(minus), 1st Anti-Tank
Bn., 1st Tank Bn.,
comprising 3rd Platoon and
a heavy section of 1st
Platoon, making a total of
eight vehicles. The Ontos
fired an average of 50–60
rounds per day; to increase
the inadequate internal basic
load of 12 rounds, the seats
were removed to
accommodate an extra 15 or
so, with the gunner sitting on
a pile of ammunition. In
action, vehicle commanders
fired their .30 cal. machine
guns and .50 cal. spotting
rifles at the target area as
they moved down the streets,
to prevent accurate return
fire by the enemy RPG-2s
and 57mm recoilless rifles.
The 106mm rifles were fired
single shot or two at a time

but not in salvoes of six.
After firing, the vehicles
quickly turned away from
the target and moved
rapidly to safe positions
behind friendly lines where
they were reloaded for the
next assignment. (USMC
A190473)

ABOVE
The brunt of the fighting in
Hue was borne by the
Vietnamese.
Three USMC and 11
ARVN battalions were used
against the enemy force of
approximately 10,000 men.
As a point of honour the
ARVN, including elements
of 7th Armd. Cavalry Regt.,
led the counter-attack
against the enemy
entrenched in the Citadel.
On 24 February the
Imperial Palace was finally
captured, but mopping–up
operations continued until 2
March. (Armor Magazine)

Coastguard mission to interdict enemy supplies and reinforcements infiltrating South Vietnam by sea. As NVA forces increased in strength, III MAF could no longer afford the luxury of leaving tank and Ontos platoons afloat when its armor assets on land were so limited and they were gradually phased back to their parent organisations.

SLF operations continued until September 1969, by which time 62 landings had been made on the Vietnamese coastline. The enemy never chose to do more than lightly harass a landing. There were no classic beach assaults with amtracs in the van, and no battles fought at the water's edge in true Marine style. However, the Marines did deny freedom of movement to the enemy in coastal areas and, perhaps most importantly, maintained and enhanced the doctrine of amphibious operations which remains the primary mission of the US Marine Corps.

5 AUSTRALIAN ARMOR IN VIETNAM

During the 1960s the Royal Australian Armoured Corps (RAAC) represented only four per cent of the Australian Army's strength. In August 1962 a team of jungle warfare specialists was despatched to Vietnam; but in the early years of Australia's military involvement there was no requirement for AFVs, notwithstanding their successful use in the jungles of New Guinea and Borneo during the Second World War. After the commitment of American ground troops, Australia followed suit with the deployment of 1st Battalion, Royal Australian Regiment (RAR), together with signals and logistic support elements, in June 1965. The battalion was located at Bien Hoa under operational control of the US 173rd Airborne Brigade.

The first RAAC unit arrived with this contingent. The Australian Logistic Support Company included eight M113A1 APCs manned by members of 1 Troop, A Squadron, 4th/19th Prince of Wales's Light Horse. In the absence of any official title other than 'RAAC detachment' they retained their unit designation but were commonly referred to by their nickname—'The Ponies'. In September 1965, the unit was increased to a full-strength APC troop of 13 M113A1s. Two M125A1 81mm mortar carriers were added for increased fire support. As the only armored element in the battalion group its vehicles were in constant demand, and often acted as 'light tanks' in the assault when support by American tanks was not available. In March 1966 the 'RAAC detachment' became officially known as 1st APC Troop.

In the same month the Australian government announced a substantial increase in Australia's contribution to the war with the formation of 1st Australian Task Force (1 ATF) comprising two infantry battalions (5 and 6 RAR) plus additional combat support elements. Among these was 1st APC Squadron, which relieved 1st

APC Troop. It consisted of a squadron headquarters, an administrative troop, two APC troops and a support company troop. Standard equipment was the diesel-powered M113A1, together with special-purpose variants based on the same chassis. This highly reliable and versatile vehicle performed admirably, and its amphibious capability allowed it to negotiate most streams and paddyfields without difficulty. Armament comprised a single .50 cal. M2HB Browning on a pintle mount. Soon after arrival, gunshields were fabricated by 106th Field Workshops, RAEME, giving partial protection against hostile fire. Subsequently, many APCs were fitted with fully enclosed machine gun turrets.

1st Australian Task Force was placed under control of II Field Force and was allotted its own TAOR in Phuoc Tuy Province southeast of Saigon. The 1 ATF base camp was established in a rubber plantation at Nui Dat just north of the provincial capital, Baria. As the only armored support for the task force, 1st APC Squadron was hard pressed to meet the continual demands of the infantry battalions with only two APC troops. At this time an APC troop comprised three sabre sections, each of three APCs, and a troop headquarters of four.

By reducing the number of APCs in each troop from 13 to 11, by employing the ambulances as standard APCs, and by incorporating vehicles from the support company troop, it was possible to create a third APC troop. Each APC section could lift a platoon, while the infantry company headquarters was carried by the troop headquarters vehicles. Two of the troops were usually under operational control of infantry battalions at any one time. Because the support company of the battalion usually moved by helicopter, the support company troop of APCs was seldom used in its orthodox role. Instead the six 'mortar tracks' were generally paired off into three sections of two vehicles, and each section was attached to one of the existing APC troops.

After the establishment of the base camp at Nui Dat, 1 ATF undertook counter-guerilla operations throughout Phuoc Tuy Province. The APCs were used for a multiplicity of missions and became the workhorses of the task force, being nicknamed the 'Road Runners'. They transported infantry to and from operational areas; they were used for logistical tasks, resupplying infantry units in the field or evacuating captured equipment and stores; they deployed artillery to fire support bases; they inserted and extracted SAS patrols; they acted as a communications link for artillery and aerial fire support; they served as mobile base-plates for mortars, and for medical evacuation, and as part of the Ready Reaction Force at Nui Dat. In the latter role, the squadron was frequently called out at immediate notice to go to the aid of a Provincial Government Post that was under attack or to support an infantry ambush which had made contact and was in need of assistance. One APC troop was always assigned to this duty, and its response became so rapid that on receiving a call the troop was driving through the main gate of the task force area within three minutes. On one occasion when the alarm hooter sounded at night the troop forged down the road only to find the gate still padlocked—so the APCs simply drove through it!

In addition to their role as troop transports the APCs were employed as cavalry for route security, convoy escort, recon-

While clearing a helicopter landing zone near Route 15 in November 1966, 'Two-two Alpha' struck a mine, sustaining damage to the drive sprocket and front roadwheels. The crew escaped without injury. Royal Australian Electrical and Mechanical Engineers (RAEME) undertake repairs with the aid of their M113A1 'Fitters' Track'. This versatile vehicle was organic to the Light Aid Detachments (LAD) assigned to APC and tank squadrons. In 1969 Australian APCs were fitted with supplementary armor under the hull and sponsons. The 'belly armor' kit, produced in Australia, comprised a steel plate $\frac{1}{2}$in. thick at the front, reducing to $\frac{3}{8}$in. at the back. (AWM FOR/66/529/VN)

Carriers of 1st APC Sqn. move through the rubber plantation at Long Tan on 19 August 1966, the day after the epic battle in which 'Delta' Co., 6 RAR, defeated a reinforced battalion of 275th VC Regt. in pouring rain, inflicting losses of 245 killed, 500 wounded and three captured at a cost of 18 dead and 21 wounded. The APCs of 3 Troop, 1st APC Sqn. joined the battle at a critical moment, bringing timely reinforcements and routing two enemy companies as they formed up to attack the beleagured infantry of 'Delta' Company. In this one action the Australians killed more of the enemy than they had in the preceding 14 months since their arrival. With their bizarre brand of gallows humour the Australians promptly named the battle Operation 'Smithfield', after the famous London meat market. (AWM CUN/66/698/VN)

'UBETCHA', an M113A1 of 1 Troop, B Sqn., 3rd Cavalry Regt. moves through the coastal village of Lang Phuoc Hai in the south of Phuoc Tuy Province. The T-50 turret was fitted to Australian APCs from 1968. It mounted either one .50 cal. M2HB and one .30cal. L3A3 Browning, or twin .30 cal. guns. At first the T-50 frequently jammed because the ceramic balls of the turret race disintegrated due to vehicle vibration or violent cross-country movement. This was overcome by inserting shims to balance the turret exactly. The .30/.50 cal. combination proved unsatisfactory in its conventional configuration because the .50 cal. lay so close to the turret wall that it was both inaccessible for servicing and difficult to cock. Most crews subsequently moved it to the right-hand aperture and mounted the .30 cal. on the turret roof, as shown in the photograph. Similarly, with the twin .30 cal. combination, crews retained one L3A3 in the turret for firing under armor and fitted the other with pistol-grip trigger on a pintle mounting above the turret for greater flexibility (in this configuration the Browning was designated L3A4). Spare .30 cal. ammunition boxes were stowed in a rack along the roof of the APC, while the two minigun boxes at the rear contained twelve M18A1 Claymore mines. (Directorate of Armour, RAAC)

naissance, perimeter defence, 'cordon and search' operations and as fire support during infantry operations. One technique that proved successful was the APC Ambush. This was undertaken by any number of carriers from three to 13, with or without infantry assistance. The essentials were thorough preparation and reconnaissance, a cover plan designed to conceal intentions rather than presence, and a lot of patience. The killing zone was covered by the weapons of every vehicle which could bear, but primary reliance was placed on a concentration of anything from 20 to 40 Claymore mines which could be fired from any of two vehicles in the ambush. The APCs undertook cavalry tasks far more frequently than the orthodox troop-carrying role.

In January 1967, following a re-organisation of the RAAC, 1st APC Squadron became A Squadron, 3rd Cavalry Regiment. Despite their success, the APCs had their limitations. They were unable to force their way through dense jungle or bamboo, and their firepower was insufficient to destroy enemy fortified bunkers. For these tasks tanks were needed; and in October 1967 the Australian government decided to send a squadron of Centurion tanks and a third infantry battalion to Vietnam.

The decision provoked considerable criticism in Parliament and certain other uninformed quarters, as indicated in this editorial in the 'Sydney Herald' which, while endorsing the provision of another infantry battalion, went on: 'It is much more difficult to imagine what use will be found for the squadron of Centurion tanks. These tanks, which were designed for desert warfare [sic], are too heavy and cumbersome for fighting in jungle and paddy. One suspects they will be used chiefly for perimeter defence as mobile pillboxes.' Even in the Army, many doubted the viability of tanks despite their widespread use by American forces in Vietnam. Accordingly, only a 'half' squadron was deployed, since the tanks had to prove themselves before armor strength was augmented.

The Centurions of C Squadron, 1st Armoured Regiment landed at Vung Tau on 24 February 1968. The unit comprised a squadron headquarters of two command tanks, two troops of four tanks each,

LEFT
*Centurions of C Sqn.,
1st Armoured Regt. are
loaded aboard SS
Japerit, bound for
South Vietnam. In
October 1967 the
Centurion tanks
destined for Vietnam
were modified at 3rd
Base Workshops,
Bandiana, with
additional armor on the
glacis plate, infra-red
night driving and
fighting equipment, a
No. 4 RCP ballistic
sight, a 100-gallon
auxiliary fuel tank at
the rear and a .50 cal.
ranging gun co-axial to
the 20pdr. main guns;
and then designated
Centurion Mark 5/1
(Australian). The
vehicle callsign number
was applied to the
bazooka plates and
transmission covers in
broad white tape for
administrative purposes
when loading and
unloading. On arrival
in Vietnam it was
impossible to service the
Centurions, since the
wharfside workers in
Sydney had stolen the
tools from every tank!
(1st Armoured
Regiment, RAAC)*

ABOVE
*Centurion tanks
disembark from an
LCU at the Song Dinh
hard near Baria soon
after their arrival in
Vietnam, February
1968. M113A1 APCs
of A Sqn., 3rd Cavalry
Regt. stand by to escort
the tanks to the Task
Force Headquarters at
Nui Dat. The
Centurions are
complete with bazooka
plates, trackguards,
spare track links and
headlight assemblies on
the glacis plate—all*

*were soon to be
discarded or ripped off
by the jungle. (Peter
De Jong)*

BELOW
*Following an assault on
an enemy bunker system
during Operation
'Pinaroo', the two
Centurion armored
recovery vehicles
(ARV) of C Sqn.
LAD section were
modified with armored
plates welded to the
rear tool bins protecting
stores and personnel
such as engineer 'mini-*

*teams' and tracker dog
teams carried on the
rear decks. Here 'Nine-
eight Bravo',
Centurion ARV Mk. 2
(169112) halts during
Operation 'Cooktown
Orchid', April 1968.
To the rear is an
M113A1 'Fitters'
Track', an M577A1,
standard M113A1
APCs and a Centurion
Bridgelayer with its
bridge raised on struts
to allow access to the
engine compartment.
(Peter De Jong)*

ABOVE
The tank squadron in Vietnam was supported by a Special Equipment Troop of two Centurion Mk. 5 Bridgelayers and two Centurion Mk. 5 Tankdozers. These vehicles enhanced the mobility of an armored unit by spanning or clearing obstacles on the battlefield. Other ingenious uses were found, including employment as a troop transport in relatively safe areas. This form of travel was not favoured by Australian troops, as its wallowing induced motion sickness. However, a complete company of ARVN infantry could be carried in the inverted bridge. A Centurion Bridgelayer forms a convenient landing pad for a Sioux H-13 helicopter, nicknamed 'Possum', of 161 (Independent) Reconnaissance Flight during Operation 'Cooktown Orchid', April 1968. This technique was employed for emergency casualty evacuation, liaison or resupply where vegetation made more conventional landings impossible without damaging rotor blades. The 'Possums' gave navigational assistance to armored units operating in thick, featureless country, and early warning of marshy ground and obstacles. (Peter De Jong)

BELOW
Centurions Mk. 5/1 (Aust) of 1 Troop, C Sqn., 1st Armoured Regt., stand guard on Route 2, south of Binh Ba, as a land clearing team of 1st Field Squadron, Royal Australian Engineers (RAE) uproots rubber trees by means of marine anchor chain towed between two bulldozers. Trees were cleared to a distance of 200 metres either side of roads, denying ambush positions to the enemy. (Peter De Jong)

two armored recovery vehicles, two bridgelayers, two tankdozers, and a forward delivery troop of three replacement tanks. The Centurions first saw action in March during Operation 'Pinaroo' when they gave fire support to a task force search-and-destroy action in the Long Hai Hills, a long-established Viet Cong refuge in the south of Phuoc Tuy Province.

During 'Pinaroo' and subsequent operations around the Long Hai Hills, C Squadron encountered many unforeseen problems of operating tanks in such hostile terrain—exterior fittings were torn off by trees and vines; mud compacted under bazooka plates, clogging suspension components to a degree which defied maintenance procedures and caused such rolling resistance that performance was impaired; engine compartments and exhaust pipes became covered with torn-off vegetation, which subsequently dried and then burst into flames. Tank crews quickly overcame these difficulties, but operations were hampered by a totally inadequate allocation of spare parts. Within a month the three replacement tanks had been cannibalised to keep the others running. At one time C Squadron was reduced to a single spare clutch in Vietnam.

In May most of 1 ATF moved to Bien Hoa Province, where it took part in Operation 'Toan Thang' to counter the enemy 'mini-Tet' offensive against Saigon. Two fire support bases, 'Coogee' and 'Coral', were established astride Route 16 on the boundary of Binh Duong and Bien Hoa Provinces to interdict enemy movement towards the capital. FSB 'Coral' was occupied late on 13 May, so its defences were incomplete when the enemy attacked in battalion strength in the early hours of the following morning. The only armor present was a section of mortar tracks, and the assault was contained only with difficulty. On the next day, 1 and 2 Troops and

'Nine-two Alpha', a Centurion Tankdozer, is towed to safety after hitting a mine outside Camp Blackhorse, the home of 11 ACR near Xuan Loc, during the advance of 1 and 2 Troops, C Sqn. from Nui Dat to Fire Support Bases 'Coral' and 'Balmoral', May 1968. The mine, obviously intended for an AFV of 11 ACR, destroyed the front right suspension unit and roadwheels. This was the first occasion that a Centurion struck a mine in Vietnam. The damage was repaired within 18 hours. This vehicle, 169106, fired the first Centurion main armament round in Vietnam during Operation 'Pinaroo'. (AWM ERR/68/534/VN)

The crew of Centurion 'Three-two Bravo' relax among shady rubber trees at their Nui Dat, base camp, July 1968. After Operation 'Pinaroo' the bazooka plates were removed because mud and vegetation compacted beneath them, causing distortion and damage to the trackguards and stowage bins. The accumulated matter around the suspension could immobilise the tank eventually. Roadwheels and suspension units proved capable of absorbing RPG-2 attack without hull penetration. The discarded bazooka plates were cut up as gunshields, or else used for cooking steaks during barbeques at 'the Dat'.

Spare roadwheels were attached to the glacis plate by means of 'Omega brackets'—a field modification to simplify resupply after mine damage or extended running on roads, when high temperatures caused shedding of the rubber tyres of the roadwheels. (AWM ERR/68/707/VN)

ABOVE RIGHT
APCs of 3 Troop, B Sqn., 3rd Cavalry Regt. sweep through the village of Binh Ba on 6 June 1969 during the most decisive engagement fought by Australian armor in Vietnam. Note that the unsatisfactory M28C sight of the T50 turret has been removed (a simple blade

vane was often substituted), and the Kalashnikov assault rifle; automatic weapons were carried externally to guard against fleeting targets to flanks and rear because of the slow manual traverse of the turret. (AWM BEL/69/386/VN)

BELOW RIGHT
At the height of the battle of Binh Ba, 6 June 1969, the Centurions and APCs supporting 'Delta' Co., 5 RAR opened fire into the rubber plantation to the west of the village just as an enemy company was forming up to counter-attack. Captured documents later revealed that the enemy suffered 75 per cent casualties. A Centurion of B

Sqn. engages the treeline with co-axial machine gun fire during this action. (AWM BEL/69/382/VN)

headquarters elements of A Squadron, 3rd Cavalry Regiment arrived to bolster the defences of 'Coral'. The position was attacked again by an NVA regiment on the night of 16 May, and the perimeter was penetrated in several places, but the APCs' firepower and ability to manoeuvre under fire proved decisive in stemming the determined assault.

Once established in the area, the infantry companies conducted patrols in the surrounding jungle to root out enemy camps. On 23 May the Centurions of C Squadron arrived at FSB 'Coral' to increase the offensive strength of the task force. A further FSB named 'Balmoral' was established some 6,000 yards north of 'Coral', and on 25 May B Company, 1 RAR and the Centurions of 2 Troop occupied the position after a brisk firefight against an enemy-defended locality during the march from 'Coral'.

The enemy reacted violently to the threat of 'Balmoral'. It was attacked at 0400hrs on 26 May by an NVA battalion-sized force, and again two nights later by a full NVA regiment. Both assaults withered under the combined firepower of infantry small arms, supporting artillery, air strikes and tank guns firing canister. In the second attack the tanks proved useful in a number of ways besides their devastating firepower. The troop leader, Lt. Mick Butler, assisted target indication for air strikes by creating a fire co-ordination line with the tracer ammunition of his tank's .50 cal. ranging gun. Cpl. 'Bluey' Lowe, commanding 'Three-two Charlie', transmitted corrections to the artillery controller at 'Coral' who was directing supporting fire from surrounding bases. The attack persisted for several hours before the enemy withdrew at dawn. During the assault the four Centurions had each fired approximately 50 rounds of 20pdr. canister and HE to considerable effect, and the ground forward of their positions was strewn with enemy dead. At first light two Centurions moved out to clear any enemy remaining around the perimeter. Several prisoners were taken; but after an Australian medic was wounded by a hand grenade while tending enemy casualties no quarter was given, and any further resistance was crushed under the tracks of the tanks.

Meanwhile at 'Coral' the Centurions of 1 Troop fought a successful action against a bunker system on 26 May. Two days later 1 Troop was called to the assistance of C Company, 1 RAR, trapped under heavy fire from a bunker complex in thick jungle. C Company was conducting a patrol operation with APCs of A Squadron, 3rd Cavalry Regiment, and had dismounted in the face of jungle which the APCs were unable to penetrate. The troop leader, Lt. Gerry McCormack, 'scrambled' his three tanks; but two broke down before leaving 'Coral', and one of the two SHQ tanks provided as replacements also suffered mechanical problems (indicative of the acute shortage of spares). McCormack elected to proceed with just his own and the remaining Centurion, an ARV and the 'Fitters' Track'.

At the scene of the contact, the APCs were vainly trying to break through the jungle to the men of C Company, who were steadily being encircled. The Centurions crashed into the jungle, carving a track through the trees for the APCs and themselves. Moving with the utmost care because of the wounded littering the ground, the Centurions jockeyed into position and then opened fire with

canister. C Company had been ambushed in the heart of a battalion position, and the tanks were taking fire from several directions. Indeed, after an RPG exploded in the trees above his head and was followed by a stream of automatic fire, McCormack was unable to locate its source and demanded on the infantry net: 'Where's it coming from?' The answer came back: 'There's a bloke in the trench below you—don't look down!' McCormack quickly silenced the fire by dropping two No. 36 grenades over the side of the turret into the trench.

The tanks moved slowly forward, destroying more bunkers; at one point two enemy infantrymen rose up out of a weapons pit just as a Centurion opened fire with canister at a range of 30 yards—nothing remained except some bloody shoes. The Centurions subdued the bunkers by firing canister to strip away the vegetation, followed by APCBC solid shot to destroy the position. Even the tank drivers employed personal weapons, including M79 grenade launchers, against targets masked from the view of crewmen in the turrets. For

40 minutes the two tanks moved back and forth, firing round after round into enemy positions, while C Company retrieved their dead and wounded and climbed aboard the APCs under continual mortar and small arms fire.

The Australians were then ordered to withdraw; but this created a dilemma, as the quickest exit was along the track made by the tanks, which risked freshly planted mines. At that moment American gunships came up on the radio net: 'Hello Aussie tankers, this is Playboy two-three. I'm above you now. Can I be of assistance?' 'Too right! Anything forward of my gun barrel is unfriendly,' replied the troop leader. With a laconic 'Roger that' the Cobras of 334th Armed Helicopter Company ('Playboys') swept into action, 'prepping the treeline' either side of the track with minigun fire as the APCs safely withdrew, followed by the Centurions with their guns pointing rearwards.

C Company, 1 RAR escaped annihilation at the hands of the enemy thanks to the devastating firepower of the two Centurions. Their determined intervention was an object lesson in the effective use of armored vehicles in Vietnam, irrespective of the forbidding terrain and conditions that prevailed. The tank actions during Operation 'Toan Thang' put paid to the theories of armchair critics as to the viability of the Centurion in tropical warfare.

After the battles at 'Coral' and 'Balmoral' 1 ATF returned to Phuoc Tuy Province. A third Centurion troop was formed early in May from the two SHQ tanks and the two tankdozers. In September the tanks of 3 and 4 Troops arrived in Vietnam, bringing C Squadron

On 20 November 1970 virtually all the AFVs of 1 ATF were gathered at Nui Dat to commemorate Cambrai, the First World War battle celebrated as the birthday of the RAAC. In the largest congregation of Australian armor ever massed in South Vietnam, 29 Centurions of A Sqn., 1st Armoured Regt., and 38 APCs of B Sqn., 3rd Cavalry Regt., took part in the parade. The photograph illustrates almost all the modifications made to Centurions to suit the Vietnam theatre of operations. A stowage rack on the turret top rear contains ten boxes of .30 cal. ammunition for the commander's machine gun, and an AN/PRC-25 man-pack radio; as the American radios used by the infantry had a different frequency band to that of the British B47 tank/infantry set it was necessary for the tank commander to have a radio of similar capability. The trackguards are cut back front and rear and the stowage bins reinforced to prevent mud from clogging the suspension and trees from damaging the bins. Water jerrycans are stowed across the transmission covers, and the stowage basket holds cans of oil and C-ration cartons. The exhaust silencer covers are fitted with mudscrapers fabricated from engineer stakes: crew members cleaned their boots when mounting the tank to prevent mud being deposited inside the turret. The mudscrapers were welded at an exact distance apart so that C-ration cans could be wedged between them: at the end of a day's operation, the residual engine heat provided a hot meal within minutes. By 1970 the call sign plate no longer indicated the squadron—since there was only one 'in-country'. The number identifies the troop and the letter the tank within the troop—1B being the troop corporal's tank of 1 Troop. The knight chessman was an unofficial troop insignia. Note the vehicle callsign is repeated on the fume extractor for identification from the flanks. A total of 58 Centurions served in Vietnam during three and a half years of operations: 42 sustained damage in battle, and six hulls were damaged beyond repair. Two crewmen were killed in mine incidents. (AWM FAI/70/852/VN)

to a full strength establishment of four troops each of four Centurions. The SHQ tanks and tankdozers acted as a fifth troop for increased flexibility. Even so, the squadron's slender resources were stretched to the limit to support three infantry battalions, and it was rarely possible to allot more than one troop to any operation. A troop was invariably assigned to the Ready Reaction Force.

In February 1969 C Squadron was relieved by B Squadron, 1st Armoured Regiment. When not actively in support of infantry operations the tanks conducted reconnaissance missions throughout the province, codenamed 'Tango'. A 'Tango Force' consisted of up to two tank troops, one APC troop, two mortar tracks, an M577A1, and either an Australian infantry platoon or a company of ARVN infantry. 'Tango Forces' had the mobility and firepower to deal with any enemy encountered. The mission was simply to search and destroy in an area of operations approximately 25 by 25 kilometres, containing any manner of terrain.

Through the perseverance of their crews the Centurions were able to travel over most of the province in the dry season and even in the monsoon, to almost every area where they were needed. The tanks could negotiate terrain impassable to APCs, forcing their way through dense jungle to uncover enemy camps and bunkers. Fuel consumption was gauged at four gallons a mile, but rose to 12 gallons a mile through thick bamboo. Growing in clumps with shoots up to six inches in diameter, the resilient bamboo defied the passage of APCs, which rode up the stems until their tracks revolved helplessly in the air. The progress of tanks was only possible by battering repeatedly against the bamboo until it shattered, showering the crews with razor-sharp slivers—and with clouds of pollen, to the misery of hayfever sufferers. In this way tanks advanced some 15 yards at a time; it was then necessary to back off and clear the vegetation covering the tanks and fouling the running gear. Such slow progress

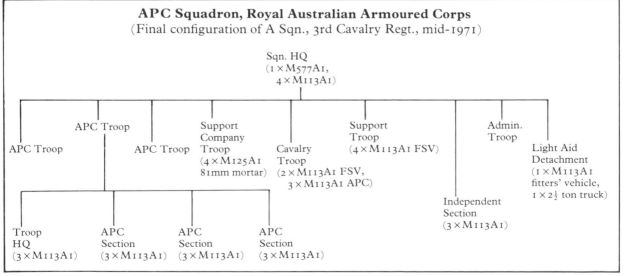

APC Squadron, Royal Australian Armoured Corps
(Final configuration of A Sqn., 3rd Cavalry Regt., mid-1971)

Sqn. HQ
(1×M577A1,
4×M113A1)

APC Troop

APC Troop

APC Troop

Support
Company
Troop
(4×M125A1
81mm mortar)

Cavalry
Troop
(2×M113A1 FSV,
3×M113A1 APC)

Support
Troop
(4×M113A1 FSV)

Admin.
Troop

Light Aid
Detachment
(1×M113A1
fitters' vehicle,
1×2½ ton truck)

Troop
HQ
(3×M113A1)

APC
Section
(3×M113A1)

APC
Section
(3×M113A1)

APC
Section
(3×M113A1)

Independent
Section
(3×M113A1)

often allowed the enemy to withdraw from prepared positions in face of the tanks.

One of the most successful actions of Australian armor in Vietnam occurred on 6 June 1969. A VC/NVA force occupied the village of Binh Ba on Route 2, three miles north of Nui Dat, fortifying many of its buildings, which were of masonry roofed with tiles. The reaction by 1 ATF was rapid and vigorous. As all the infantry companies in the surrounding area were committed, the Ready Reaction Force— comprising a composite troop of B Squadron, 1st Armoured Regiment; 3 Troop, B Squadron, 3 Cavalry Regiment; and D Company, 5 RAR—was called out immediately. Under intense RPG and small arms fire the tanks and APCs assaulted the entrenched enemy. The Centurions engaged strongpoints with HE rounds and, when these ran short, fired canister into the roofs of houses, bringing the tiles crashing down on those below. Buildings collapsed under the impact of APCBC rounds into their foundations; doors and windows were ripped out by co-axial machine gun fire and the .50 cal. rounds of the ranging guns. In four hours of savage fighting the enemy lost 99 killed, while RAAC casualties were six tank and two APC crewmen wounded. Three Centurions were badly damaged but remained in action throughout the battle.

Thereafter, the enemy generally vacated their positions rather than engage the Centurions in battle; but many successful actions were fought against bunker complexes in support of infantry operations. Few 'Diggers' will deny the value of tank support in jungle warfare. Pinned down under heavy fire before a heavily entrenched enemy, many infantrymen had cause to be thankful for the assistance given by the lumbering Centurions as they forged through dense jungle, cutting swathes through the undergrowth with canister, and crushing bunkers under their tracks or pounding them to destruction with solid shot. No longer were RAAC units derisively nicknamed 'the Koala Bears' ('not to be exported or shot at'): and their contribution in Vietnam was out of all proportion to their four per cent of the Army's manpower.

RAAC UNITS IN VIETNAM	
'RAAC Detachment'	25 May 1965–13 September 1965
1st APC Troop	14 September 1965–31 March 1966
1st APC Squadron	1 April 1966–15 January 1967
redesignated as	
A Squadron, 3rd Cavalry Regiment	16 January 1967–12 May 1969
	7 January 1971–12 March 1972
B Squadron, 3rd Cavalry Regiment	13 May 1969–6 January 1971
A Squadron, 1st Armoured Regiment	23 December 1969–16 December 1970
B Squadron, 1st Armoured Regiment	11 February 1969–22 December 1969
C Squadron, 1st Armoured Regiment	24 February 1968–10 February 1969
	17 December 1970–30 September 1971

6 ARMOR OF THE NORTH VIETNAMESE ARMY

A North Vietnamese armored force was created in October 1959. As with so many client states of the Soviet Union, its first tanks were T-34/85s—these are remanufactured models incorporating T-54 style wheels, night driving equipment and uprated engines. Tank crews relax between exercises during celebrations to mark the 25th Anniversary of the Democratic Republic of Vietnam. On the external fuel tank, the event is recorded with the dates 1945–1970. Most T-34/85s were used for training and few were encountered below the DMZ. (Nihon Denpa)

For a war that lasted 30 years and featured such a large number of AFVs, there were remarkably few occasions when combat between tanks actually occurred. The primary factor was the reluctance of the North Vietnamese to employ their armored units. It remains an enigma why the NVA, which was renowned for exploiting the capabilities of every weapon at its disposal to the full, did not make more use of its tanks until so late in the war.

It is impossible to verify how many times North Vietnamese AFVs appeared on the battlefields of South Vietnam. The first successful action by NVA armor was against Lang Vei Special Forces camp on the night of 6/7 February 1968, during the Tet offensive, when the nearby Marine base at Khe Sanh was besieged. Shortly before midnight 13 PT-76 amphibious tanks spearheaded an assault on the camp, which was held by 24 Green Berets and some 500 irregulars. The defenders fought back with a few anti-tank weapons at their disposal, including M72 LAWs (Light Anti-tank Weapon). Many of the LAWs were defective and failed to penetrate the thin armor of the PT-76. Outnumbered and heavily outgunned, the defenders fell back; the tanks, despite losses, forged on, systematically destroying bunker after bunker at point blank range. Throughout the night and far into the next day the resolute defenders held on, as their own artillery fire and air strikes deliberately pounded the position. When it proved impossible to reinforce them with units from Khe Sanh Combat Base, the few survivors broke out and were finally airlifted to safety.

The US Marine Corps must take the credit for the first tank-versus-tank action. In mid-1968 an airborne Forward Air Controller

LEFT
*Crewmen of 1st
Platoon, Co. B, 1/69th
Armor inspect a
PT-76 amphibious
tank of 202nd Armored
Regt. on the day after
the abortive assault by
NVA tanks on the Ben
Het Special Forces
camp, 4 March 1970.
This was the only
occasion that US
Army and NVA tanks
clashed during the
Vietnam War. This
PT-76 is a standard
production model with
the later D-56TM
76.2mm gun. (US
Army SC652805)*

BELOW LEFT
*Type 63 amphibious
tanks carrying NVA
infantry cross the Cua
Viet River near Dong
Ha during the 1972
offensive. The Type 63
was a Chinese-built
derivative of the
PT-76 with a modified
hull and a new turret,
similar in shape to that
of the T-54, mounting
an 85mm gun. Many
tanks identified as
PT-76s on the
battlefields of South
Vietnam were in fact
Chicom Type 63s.
(Nihon Denpa)*

RIGHT
*An early production
series T-54 leads a
column of NVA tanks
during the 1972
offensive. Throughout
the campaign, NVA
armor violated many of
the basic tenets of
armored warfare:
vulnerable to air
attack, tanks moved in
close column when the
situation demanded
dispersal; in the
assault, tanks were
committed in small
numbers without
infantry or artillery
support. They suffered
heavy losses as a result.
(Nihon Denpa)*

(FAC) codenamed 'Southern Charlie' spotted a PT-76 being washed in the Ben Hai River in the DMZ. Its location was radioed to Con Thien, where an M48A3 of 3rd Platoon, A Company, 3rd Tank Battalion fired three rounds of HE (delay) 'burst-on-target' at extreme range, with 'Southern Charlie' adjusting. The third round struck the PT-76, and the crew fled. Subsequently some homeward-bound F4 Phantoms with ordnance to spend pounded the tank to scrap, and, predictably, claimed the kill—but it had been a remarkable feat of tank gunnery.

The NVA armor put in another appearance on the foggy night of 3 March 1969 in an attack on a Special Forces camp at Ben Het in the Central Highlands. PT-76s and BTR-50 APCs of 16th Company, 4th Bn., 202nd Armored Regt. were tasked with the destruction of the camp's battery of M107 SP guns; but apart from the three CIDG companies and their 'Green Beret' advisers, Ben Het was also defended by two M42A1 Dusters and by the Pattons of 1st Ptn., B Co., 1/69 Armor. Hearing the squeal of approaching tanks, the tankers loaded with HEAT rounds; but in the fog the Xenon searchlights proved useless, and it was not until a PT-76 struck a mine and then began firing that the Patton gunners spotted a target. The first gunner to fire, Spec.4 Frank Hembree, sighted on the muzzle flashes and destroyed the PT-76 with his second shot.

Flares soon revealed the tanks to each other, and an NVA gunner scored an HE hit on the M48A3 of Sgt. Havermale. The company commander, Capt. John Stovall, was standing on the rear deck, and the driver was manning an externally-mounted machine gun. The driver was killed, as was the loader, and Havermale and Stovall were both blown off the tank and ten feet to the rear, although there was no penetration damage. The firefight continued; the Patton crews soon ran out of their small supply of HEAT, and substituted HE rounds with concrete-piercing fuses. A second PT-76 was destroyed before enemy fire slackened and the NVA armor withdrew, leaving two tanks and a BTR-50PK wrecked on the field.

These were the only occasions that American tanks clashed with North Vietnamese armor. Enemy AFVs were encountered a few other times in South Vietnam. A PT-76 was knocked out by a 90mm recoilless rifle during an attack on a CIDG camp at Bo Dup in 1968; another was located by a helicopter from Troop A, 1st Squadron, 9th Cavalry, on 10 February 1968 and destroyed by a tactical air strike during Operation 'Pegasus', the relief of Khe Sanh Combat Base. An unsubstantiated report suggests that late in the war an M728 CEV wrecked an NVA T-54 with a single round from its 165mm demolition gun. Doubtless, other enemy AFVs were chanced upon by LRRPs and Special Forces units during their clandestine activities when enemy base areas in South Vietnam and elsewhere were detected and then attacked from the air; some strongholds, such as those in the A Shau Valley, occasionally contained AFVs.

The first major tank-vs-tank engagements of the war occurred during 'Lam Son 719', the South Vietnamese incursion into Laos to disrupt the Ho Chi Minh Trail during February 1971. On 19 February, in the first battle between ARVN and NVA armor, five M41A3s of 1st Squadron, 11th Armored Cavalry Regiment destroyed six T-54s and 16 PT-76s without loss during an enemy attack against a fire base designated LZ31, north of Aloui. A week

Many of the medium tanks in NVA service were Chinese T-59s. Differing from it only in minor internal details, the T-59 is an unlicensed copy of the T-54A. From photographs it is almost impossible to distinguish between them, but the Notek driving light beside the standard Soviet-style ones of this tank suggests it is a T-59. South Vietnamese peasants line the road as NVA tanks advance into Quang Tri Province, 1972. (Nihon Denpa)

later NVA tanks launched another assault on LZ31. The first and second waves were repulsed with the aid of US tactical air strikes, but three T-54s finally gained the summit of the position, forcing the defenders to withdraw. This was the major achievement of enemy tanks during 'Lam Son 719'.

After the loss of LZ31 further engagements took place, ARVN cavalry units destroyed approximately 30 AFVs for the loss of nine ACAVs, but enemy armor was now present in strength. Despite reinforcements from Military Region I, the maximum ARVN armor strength in Laos at any one time was only three M41A3 squadrons less two troops, and six armored cavalry assault squadrons. Menaced by superior forces and the prospect of the April rains, the incursion was curtailed and a withdrawal began on 19 March. Lack of co-ordination at high command levels hampered the retreat at every turn. Much operational equipment was abandoned as units fell back over difficult terrain, constantly hounded by the enemy. Although the enemy launched no major offensive for the remainder of 1971, traffic along the Ho Chi Minh Trail was only briefly disrupted.

Throughout 1971 US forces were redeployed as the process of 'Vietnamisation' accelerated. By the end of the year 54 per cent of the remaining US combat battalions were armored units, reflecting the importance now attached to AFVs. The last American armored unit—1st Squadron, 1st Cavalry—departed in April 1972.

The NVA was not idle during this time. Large quantities of modern conventional weapons were obtained from the Eastern bloc to offset the superior firepower of the South Vietnamese. Biding his time until all US ground forces had left, the enemy built up extensive stockpiles of supplies and equipment in Laos, Cambodia and South Vietnam itself.

With the scheduled departure in August 1971 of the US 1st Brigade, 5th Infantry Division (Mechanized) and the last remaining tank battalion, 1/77th Armor, the formation of the first South Vietnamese tank regiment equipped with M48A3 tanks was authorised on 31 July 1971. Designated 20th Tank Regiment, it was specifically organised to meet the capabilities of the ARVN and included an armored rifle company. These troops were supposed to ride the tanks to provide protection from RPG teams, but, in the event, this unit was used merely to provide replacement tank crews.

In September the regiment was issued with 54 war-weary M48A3s, which were divided into three tank squadrons and a regimental headquarters. Two of the tanks were totally unserviceable and all the remainder were in various states of disrepair. Few of the regiment's personnel had experience of armor, and many equipment deficiencies were beyond the capabilities of the untrained crews and mechanics to rectify. The problem was compounded by the lack of spare parts and by the language barrier between the US instructors and Vietnamese crewmen. Technical manuals had to be laboriously translated, creating anomalies when there was no equivalent word in the Vietnamese language, as when 'ballistic computer' was translated as 'adding machine'.

Priority was given to gunnery training, but the crews had considerable difficulty in mastering the complex fire control system and few first-round hits were obtained. The value of the coincidence rangefinder and ballistic computer was not appreciated until the regimental executive officer attained consistent hits through their proper use. Thereafter correct procedures were followed, and by 25 January 1972 41 of the 51 available crews had qualified to a standard as rigorous as that applied in US units. Considering the parlous state of the equipment and the mediocre quality of personnel, this was an impressive record. Unit tactical training continued until the end of March.

On 30 March 1972 the NVA unleashed their Easter offensive when three divisions led by approximately 100 tanks struck south across the DMZ. Defending the northern provinces were three ARVN divisions including the untested 3rd Infantry Division, and two brigades of Marines. Foul weather prevented tactical air support. The forward fire bases were overrun under the most intensive enemy artillery barrages of the war. The 3rd ARVN Division collapsed, and 20th Tank Regt. moved to Dong Ha to bolster the crumbling defences with its 42 operational tanks. On the morning of 2 April the regiment engaged the advancing enemy.

The M48A3s opened fire at ranges of 2,500 to 3,200 metres, and destroyed nine PT-76s and two T-54s—much to the bewilderment of the NVA commander, whose intercepted radio net attributed the losses to direct fire weapons which he could not locate. The 20th Tank Regt. suffered no losses in this action. Seldom has a newly formed unit acquitted itself so effectively under such a baptism of fire.

Air strikes north of the Mieu Giang River continued that

afternoon, destroying another 12 NVA tanks. That night the enemy attempted a crossing, but the Patton crews made good use of their Xenon searchlights; heavy casualties were inflicted by skilful co-ordination of lights and tank and infantry weapons, before the vulnerable lights were all destroyed by mortar and artillery fragmentation. Enemy activity was relatively light for the next few days, and ARVN troops eradicated NVA pockets south of the Mieu Giang.

For the next two weeks 20th Tank Regt. remained in blocking positions along the 'Dong Ha Line'. Numerous engagements took place with NVA armor, but the enemy became increasingly wary of the regiment's skill in tank gunnery, and the mere presence of an M48A3 was often sufficient to induce T-54s to withdraw. However, the toll of tanks and men was high, as the enemy infiltrated tank-hunter teams armed with RPGs across the river. On 23 April, the NVA employed the 9M14M *Malyutka* ('Sagger') anti-tank guided missile for the first time, destroying one M48A3 and an ACAV of the regiment's 2nd Squadron. Initially, South Vietnamese crewmen were mesmerised by the erratic flight of the missile. Its devastating terminal effect on targets was demoralising; on eight separate occasions the 'Sagger' caused a tank to explode and burn immediately. But troops soon devised counter-measures. On firing, the 'Sagger' emitted a distinctive 'signature' of grey smoke from its launch site. It was then up to its gunner to fly the wire-guided missile to its target by means of a joystick control. The solution was for every AFV other than the target vehicle to fire all weapons at an area 15 metres (the length of the joystick control wire) in all directions around the plume of smoke, to make the gunner flinch and lose control of his missile. Meanwhile the crew of the target vehicle counted to five and then manoeuvred violently in any direction, forcing the enemy to make a sudden, and perhaps ineffective, correction to his flight path.

Under cover of a massive artillery and rocket bombardment, the enemy resumed the offensive against the 'Dong Ha Line' at dawn on 27 April. The 20th Tank Regt. was so heavily engaged that by the next day only 18 tanks remained operational. These were whittled away to nothing during the bitterly contested retreat which followed, as ARVN resistance collapsed. The regiment had been wiped out in one month of combat. Used mainly in a static defensive role, it had consistently outfought its opponents, destroying at least 50 NVA tanks without losing a single M48A3 to enemy tank fire.

Within a matter of weeks the regiment received replacement tanks and personnel, and after a brief period of training returned to the fray in July during the ARVN counter-offensive which regained some of the lost territory. In the months that followed it was broken up into platoons under local infantry battalion control, and no further tank-vs-tank engagements of any note occurred.

In conjunction with the invasion across the DMZ, the NVA launched an offensive in Military Region 3 on 6 April 1972, and another in the Central Highlands the following day. Both advances made rapid progress as ARVN infantry disintegrated in the face of enemy armor. In MR3 the Communist objective was the provincial capital of An Loc, and ultimately Saigon itself. After a diversionary attack on Tay Ninh the assault on An Loc began on 13 April. Over the

Airpower had a decisive impact on the 1972 campaign, accounting for 70 per cent of NVA AFVs destroyed. Despite the deployment of mechanised air defence vehicles in support of armored units, their numbers were insufficient to counter the overwhelming superiority of the US and South Vietnamese air forces. Here ZSU-57-2 self-propelled anti-aircraft guns move into battle in the Loc Ninh sector, April 1972. The lesson was well learned, and in the 1975 offensive self-propelled AA guns were employed in considerable numbers; these included the successor to the ZSU-57-2, the formidable ZSU-23-4 Shilka. By then, however, the opposing airpower was an ineffectual force. (Nihon Denpa)

Besides the numerous AFVs supplied by the Communist bloc, the NVA used large numbers of captured vehicles, abandoned intact by the ARVN during the 1975 offensive. Estimates of NVA armor strength vary considerably, but it was of the order of 600 T-54/T-59 tanks as well as some 400 PT76/Type 63 amphibious tanks, APCs and self-propelled anti-aircraft guns. Brandishing NLF flags, NVA troops advance in a captured M41A3 and an M151A1 during the final days of the war. (Patton Cavalry Museum)

next six weeks the enemy made repeated tank attacks against the city; but most lacked co-ordinated infantry and artillery support, and they faltered before the determined resistance of ARVN tank-hunter teams armed with M72 LAWs, and Allied air support. Of an estimated 100 NVA tanks deployed in the battle for An Loc, some 80 were destroyed.

NVA armor achieved its greatest success during the offensive in the Central Highlands when 203rd Armored Regt., supported by an infantry battalion, struck the ARVN 22nd Infantry Div. at Tan Canh, which dominated Route 14 and the northern approaches to Kontum City. After a two-day artillery bombardment 18 T-54 and T-59 tanks, their headlights blazing in the morning mist, attacked from two directions at dawn on 24 April. The defenders broke and ran, abandoning their weapons as they straggled back to Kontum. That afternoon the nearby base at Dak To II was overrun by NVA tanks and infantry. For the next two weeks the NVA launched repeated tank and infantry attacks against fire support bases and Ranger camps in the surrounding area. The camps at Ben Het and Polei Kleng, astride Communist supply routes west of Kontum, bore the brunt of these attacks; Ben Het stood firm throughout the campaign but Polei Kleng fell on 9 May.

On the same day a new weapon appeared on the battlefield, when two UH-1B helicopters mounting TOW missiles destroyed three

PT-76 tanks during an assault on Ben Het Ranger camp. The introduction of the TOW and 'Sagger' anti-tank guided missiles during the 1972 fighting was destined to alter radically the future conduct of armored warfare—as evidenced a year later during the October War in the Middle East. Throughout the following three weeks of savage battle for Kontum, the TOW was a significant factor in the disruption of enemy tank attacks against the city. By the end of the month TOW missiles had registered 47 confirmed kills, including 24 tanks.

During the general counter-offensive of the following months ARVN armored cavalry regiments achieved some notable successes in combined arms operations against the enemy, confirming their superiority over their NVA counterparts in the conventional warfare that characterised the battles of the 1972 offensive. Thanks to determined ARVN resistance, massive US airpower and logistic support, the overextension of Communist forces on widely separated fronts, and their lack of co-ordination in tank attacks, the Easter offensive failed to achieve its objectives. As 1972 drew to a close both sides prepared for peace. These preparations included an enormous infusion of arms and equipment to both sides. On 28 January 1973 a ceasefire came into effect, and with it the departure of the last US forces from South Vietnam.

On 7 May 1975, the 21st anniversary of the fall of Dien Bien Phu, tanks rumbled through the streets of Saigon, now named Ho Chi Minh City, during a parade to mark the Communist victory at the conclusion of the 30-year war. In the troubled years that followed the blood-letting did not cease, and conflict still ravages South-East Asia. (Patton Cavalry Museum)

The next two years were characterised by persistent guerilla actions and 'land-grabbing' operations by both the ARVN and NVA as each side attempted to consolidate its hold over the countryside. During this period, China and the Soviet Union supplied massive shipments of war material including many AFVs. Meanwhile US military aid to South Vietnam was considerably reduced, especially in the allocation of ammunition and fuel, which slumped as a result of the oil crisis caused by the October War. By late 1974 the ARVN artillery was reduced to less than one round a gun per day. Ten squadrons of the air force were grounded for lack of spare parts. Armored units were confined to motor parks for want of fuel, ammunition and spares.

In December 1974 an NVA probing operation in Phuoc Long Province revealed the military weakness of the South Vietnamese government. The United States had assured the Republic of Vietnam of support in the event of attack. When none was forthcoming, the Communist offensive continued. Learning from their failures in the 1972 battles, NVA tanks were now closely integrated with infantry and artillery.

The South Vietnamese collapse began at Ban Me Thout in the Central Highlands. On 10 March NVA tanks overran the town and shattered the 23rd ARVN Division. President Thieu ordered a tactical withdrawal in order to protect the coastal cities and Saigon, abandoning the Central Highlands to the Communists. Retreat turned to rout; hundreds of thousands of terrified people clogged the roads in headlong flight toward the coast in what became known as the 'Convoy of Tears'. The débâcle was repeated throughout South Vietnam. In three weeks the northern two-thirds of the country was lost, and with it half of the army.

A determined stand was made at Xuan Loc, a provincial capital 38 miles north-east of Saigon. For two weeks South Vietnamese units held out against vastly superior NVA forces. They fought tenaciously, trusting in a promise from Saigon that if sufficient enemy forces were concentrated in the area the Americans would return with their overwhelming airpower. Surrounded by no less than four NVA divisions, the gallant defenders fought to the last. The B52s never came.

With the fall of Xuan Loc, South Vietnam was irretrievably lost. The Communist offensive surged to the outskirts of Saigon. On 30 April 1975 the tanks of the NVA 203rd Armored Regt. entered the city. At noon a T-54, bearing the number '843' and flying the flag of the NLF, crashed through the gates of the presidential palace. Saigon had fallen, and with it the Republic of Vietnam.

Armor played a decisive role in the Communist victory, spearheading attacks on every front in massed formations closely supported by other arms. Throughout the Vietnam War many questioned and derided the effectiveness of armored forces in South-East Asia: yet the final outcome of the conflict was decided by the use of this very weapon.

In 1954, a few thousand Frenchmen, Foreign Légionnaires, Arabs and Vietnamese had fought the bulk of the North Vietnamese Army at Dien Bien Phu with the utmost gallantry, until the position was overwhelmed after 55 days. Twenty-one years later the North Vietnamese Army overran the entire Republic of Vietnam—in just 55 days.

ACKNOWLEDGEMENTS

I wish to acknowledge the help and co-operation of many individuals and government agencies in the preparation of this book. In particular, the following have provided much invaluable material and assistance:

French Army: Col. B. de Bressy de Guast, ABC; Lt. Col. Pierre Carles, ER; Col. Michel Henry, ABC; Gén. de Brigade Henri Prèaud. Centre d'Histoire Militaire et d'Etudes de Défense Nationale; Etablissement Cinématographique et Photographique des Armées; Service Historique de l'Armée, Chateau de Vincennes.

US Army: Col. Raymond R. Battreall Jr., USA, Ret.; SFC Robert J. Burrows, USA; SFC Rodney B. Caesar, USA; SFC Gary L. Cotton, USA; Col. John S. Crow, USA; Lt. Col. George J. Dramis, USA; Maj. John P. Graber, USA, Ret.; SFC James C. Greeley, USA; Col. Stanley E. Holtom, USA, Ret.; Col. Robert J. Icks, USA; SFC Robert G. Lagana, USA; SFC Raymond J. Littmann, USA Res.; Lt. Col. James W. Loop, USA, Ret.; Lt. Col. Ronald E. Mayhew, USA; Col. Robert B. Osborn, USA, Ret.; Lt. Mike Patenaude, USA; SFC William A. Pirkle, USA; Maj. Mike D. Selvitelle, USA; SFC John N. Sewell, USA; Col. Donald P. Shaw, USA; Maj. James G. Snodgrass, USA; Lt. Col. Thomas E. White, USA; Lt. Col. Philip E. Williams, USA. Patton Museum of Cavalry and Armor; US Army Transportation Museum, Fort Eustis; US Army Military History Institute, Carlisle Barracks; US Army Armor School, Fort Knox; US Army Center of Military History, Washington DC; 11th Armored Cavalry Regiment.

US Marine Corps: Maj. W. B. 'Butch' Blackshear, USMC; Gy. Sgt. William K. Judge, USMC; Col. Bruce M. MacLaren, USMC; Maj. Ed F. McCann, USMC; Gy. Sgt. Donald J. Patnode, USMC, Ret.; Col. H. J. 'Mac' Radcliffe, USMC; Lt. Col. Claude W. Reinke, USMC; Maj. Kent R. Stone, USMC; Maj. Ky L. Thompson, USMC; Col. Oliver M. Whipple Jr., USMC; Maj. Ken W. Zitz, USMC. USMC History and Museums Division.

Australian Army: Lt. Col. P. W. Bourke, RAAC; Maj. John Burrows, RAInf.; Brig. H. J. Coates, MBE; Lt. Col. P. C. Jarratt, RAAC; WO Peter de Jong, RAEME; Maj. Roger Kershaw, RAAC; WO Doug Lennox, RAAC; WO Trevor Lowe, RAAC; Maj. Gerry McCormack, RAAC; Lt. Col. C. W. Toll, RAAC; WO Ross Shepherd, RAEME; Col. B. R. Sullivan, RAAC. Australian War Memorial.

The Editors of *Armor* Magazine, *Infantry* Magazine, *USMC Gazette*, and Col. Robert K. Brown of *Soldier of Fortune* Magazine; and Nihon Denpa.

George J. Balin; Kevin Dennigan; Kensuke Ebata; David Filsell; Michael Greenwood; Alan Guy; Paul Handel; Mike Roseberg; Pierre Touzin; Martin Windrow; and Steven J. Zaloga.

In addition, I wish to express my appreciation of the combat photographers whose work forms such an integral part of this book; and my thanks to Tim Page, one of the outstanding photographers of the war, for permission to reproduce several of his superb photographs.

Finally, I am indebted to Maj. Gen. George S. Patton for providing the introduction to *Vietnam Tracks*.

Simon Dunstan 1982

I&II Corps Tactical Zones

QUANG TRI

Dong Ha
9
Quang Tri
Khe Sanh
556
THUA THIEN
Hue
Phu Bai
1
A Shau
Da Nang
QUANG NAM
Hoi An
An Hoa
Tam ky
QUANG TIN
Chu Lai
14
QUANG NGAI
KONTUM
Quang Ngai
Dak To
1
14
Polei
Krong
Kontum
Bong Son
BINH DINH
An Khe
Pleiku
19
An Khe Pass
Qui Nhon
PLEIKU
PHU BON
1
DARLAC
14
PHU YEN
Ban Me Thuot
21
KHANH
HOA
Nha Trang
QUANG DUC
1
Gia Nghia
TUYEN DUC
Da Lat
Cam Ranh
11
1
LAN DONG
NINH
THUAN
20
Phan Rang
BINH
THUAN
1
Phan Thiet

0   50
Miles

Northern Quang Tri Province

Route 1
17th Parallel
Ben Hai River
Gio
Linh
Con
Thien
Demilitarized Zone
Leatherneck
Square
Cua Viet
River
LAOS
Rock Pile
Camp
Carroll
Cam
Lo
Dong
Ha
Quang
Tri River
Route 9
Quang
Tri
Ca Lu
Khe
Sahn
Khe Sanh Combat Base
Lang Vei